Worldview Religiou

CW01507551

Worldview Religious Studies brings the study of religion, spirituality, secularism, and other mixed attitudes of life under the overarching scheme of worldview studies. This book introduces and defines worldviews more generally before establishing a framework specific to religious studies.

The drive for meaning-making is explored through ritual-symbolic activities, ideas of 'play', and the power of emotions to transform simple ideas into values and beliefs that frame identity and signpost destiny. Identity and its sacralisation are discussed alongside gift/reciprocity theory in their relation to ideas of merit, karma, and salvation in Eastern and Western traditions. This theoretical background is used to introduce a new classification of worldviews – natural, scientific, ancestral, karmic, prophetic-sectarian, mystical, ideological, and Ludic.

Organised thematically by chapter, this book brings together familiar and unfamiliar authors, theories, and sources to challenge students and teachers of Religious Studies, Theology, and Ethics. It introduces worldview religious studies as a framework through which to re-think human endeavours to identify, cope with, and even transcend life's flaws and perils.

Douglas J Davies is Professor in the Study of Religion in the Department of Theology and Religion at Durham University, UK.

Routledge Focus on Religion

For more information about this series, please visit: www.routledge.com/
Routledge-Focus-on-Religion/book-series/RFR

Worldview Religious Studies

Douglas J Davies

Routledge
Taylor & Francis Group

LONDON AND NEW YORK

First published 2022
by Routledge
4 Park Square, Milton Park, Abingdon, Oxon OX14 4RN

and by Routledge
605 Third Avenue, New York, NY 10158

Routledge is an imprint of the Taylor & Francis Group, an informa business

© 2022 Douglas J Davies

British Library Cataloguing-in-Publication Data
A catalogue record for this book is available from the British Library

Library of Congress Cataloging-in-Publication Data
Names: Davies, Douglas J. (Douglas James), author.
Title: Worldview religious studies / Douglas J. Davies.
Description: Abingdon, Oxon; New York, NY: Routledge, 2022. |
Series: Routledge focus on religion | Includes bibliographical
references and index.
Identifiers: LCCN 2021054703 (print) | LCCN 2021054704 (ebook) |
ISBN 9781032150840 (hbk) | ISBN 9781032150864 (pbk) |
ISBN 9781003242437 (ebk)
Subjects: LCSH: Philosophy and religion. | Religion–Philosophy. | Religions.
Classification: LCC B56 .D38 2022 (print) | LCC B56 (ebook) |
DDC 201/.61–dc23/eng/20211220
LC record available at https://lccn.loc.gov/2021054703
LC ebook record available at https://lccn.loc.gov/2021054704

ISBN: 978-1-032-15084-0 (hbk)
ISBN: 978-1-032-15086-4 (pbk)
ISBN: 978-1-003-24243-7 (ebk)

DOI: 10.4324/9781003242437

Typeset in Times New Roman
by Deanta Global Publishing Services, Chennai, India

Contents

Part 1

Theories and Perspectives

Introduction

Worldviews are shared perspectives on life that emerge as the human drive for meaning creates patterns of values, beliefs, and behaviours in response to natural and existential environments. They intensify everyday life experiences through ritual-symbolic events that foster identity and creative living, integrate individuals within society, inform mind-sets and lifestyles, and help people confront and transcend life's besetting problems, especially death. Worldviews change whether slowly or through rapid revolutionary transformation.

Theory level, thinkers, and typology

Of the many potential academic framings of worldviews in economics, biology, history, law, politics, psychology, or theology, this book follows the interdisciplinary approach of Religious Studies especially drawing from anthropology and sociology, offering a provisional classification of different types of worldviews alongside high-, mid-, and low-range theories and scholars important for Religious Studies.

Thinking generally, high-range theories might include big-bang theory in cosmology, evolution in biology, continental drift in geology, the unconscious dynamics of mind in psychoanalysis, and plausibility theory in sociology, Gaia theory, and global warming in environmental studies, and Dialectical Materialism in Marxism. As for worldviews, high-level theories map how the world makes sense, how mid-range ideas spell that out, and low-range theories bring finer nuance. High-range perspectives are notable in small-scale societies and in mass populations with ideologically strong political leadership, e.g. Russia or China, but there we can also find small groups with their own worldviews existing in tension with the state, as with Jehovah's Witnesses in Russia, or some Muslim groups in China. For teaching worldviews as part of Religious Studies, some speak of Big

DOI: 10.4324/9781003242437-2

Ideas as a guiding framework, and this is reflected here in chapters two to five (Christopher, 2020:197).

Ecology and Environmentalism is fast becoming a worldview of its own while, in today's Britain, the National Health Service (NHS) might qualify as either a dominant worldview or as a mid-range expression of the Welfare State. Certainly, there is research on the rise of welfare and health systems and a corresponding decline of formal religious adherence in modern societies (Granqvist, 2020:304–19). Mid-range theories include the sacralisation of identity in sociology, attachment theory in psychology, reciprocity theory, and rites of passage in anthropology. Amongst low-range theories we might include theories of conspiracy, embodiment, and cultural intensification. Theories of music also play an enormous part in relation to most worldviews and rituals in general (Spitzer, 2021), to death (Partridge, 2015), and to the inspiration of performers who influence millions (Bostridge, 2015). So, high-, mid-, and low-range theories concern their level of abstraction and not their worth. In this book, they reflect different academic disciplines, methods of analysis, and their subject matter, showing the interdisciplinary nature of Religious Studies.

Worldview and religion as deutero-truths

The problems some people find with 'worldview' and 'religion' may be simplified by defining each as a 'deutero-truth'. Coming from Gregory Bateson's notion of deutero-learning, this refers to a 'second-order' level of abstraction ([1935] 1958:293). Roy Rappaport uses it to help explain a term that easily 'means something' within a community even though a member would be hard pressed to define it (1999:304–8). For school-teaching, Mark Chater and Luke Donnellan's comment resembles this when saying that 'to most of us, worldviews are both familiar and strange' (2020:118). Rappaport says, 'as high-level generalizations, deutero-truths are low in specificity, or are even downright vague' (1999:306). Indeed, 'meaning' is itself a profoundly complex concept at many levels of analysis not least for social science and religion (Davies, 1984). The same applies to the cognitive science of perception and 'understanding' of the world around us. In ways that are currently very imperfectly understood, each brain receives electrical impulses from key organs such as eyes, ears, nose, and skin and presents them to each person as pictures or representations of something 'real' and 'out there' even though things in the environment are 'seen', 'heard', and 'understood' differently by each person. However, society would not work and foster survival without some agreed-upon ideas.

Plural-disciplines

This book takes worldviews as overarching ways of embracing religion, spirituality, secularity, and wellbeing, acknowledging the corporate human drive to make sense of life as new political, economic, and cultural values prompt adaptation of behaviour and thought. Worldviews are shaped by and give shape to the way food, shelter, schemes of kinship, child-rearing, education, and health care are organised. So too with patterns of history, myth, scientific images, ethics and aesthetic creativity in music, dance, art, literature, and architecture. Athletic and sporting activities also make their presence felt. These mental, material, and behavioural endeavours respond to life's trials, hardships, and sense of mortality in distinctive ways, often under the controlling influence of invoked supernatural agents of 'religion'. Though the term 'religion' is sometimes academically questioned, this book retains it within its title *Worldview Religious Studies,* where 'worldview studies' is a model of knowledge qualified by the notion of religion, just as other worldview studies might be qualified through politics, economics, science, medicine, or ecology.

Being 'human-curious'

As for 'worldview' so for 'culture' and 'lifestyle', each has two forms of reference. One describes everyday 'taken for granted' actions, thoughts, and sayings. However, if circumstances prompt a group to think about itself, then they gain explicit significance and move towards the second, more abstract theorising of anthropology, sociology, or Religious Studies (Hoggart, 1996). One way of considering such self-understanding and interest in others is to think of people as being 'human-curious', with every community having wise people who exemplify this. Shamans, philosophers, theologians, and scientists, as well as myth-makers, story-tellers, novelists, film-makers, and web gamers, all do this. As do actors and heroes who perform society's prized insights. Moreover, innovators, reformers, and revolutionaries periodically transform established ways of doing things. And Worldview Religious Studies is the same, focusing on 'religion' as a form of meaning-making adopted by sizeable groups of people owning ideas of supernatural forces, gods, ancestors, spirits, or a single deity. Some scholars dislike the term 'religion', criticising it as a western intellectual term that makes sense in some historical–geographical contexts but not in others, especially if imposed on others. They sometimes prefer to speak of spirituality; of people being 'spiritual but not religious'; of secular values, folk belief, implicit religion, or of 'nones', a term designating people who tick the 'none' box in surveys on religious membership (Lee, 2014). Even these western-derived categories seldom exhaust how people think about their lives and can impose ideas on people.

Worldview conflicts, political and theological

The following chapters will include both familiar and unfamiliar theoretical ideas to encourage critical thinking in Worldview Religious Studies, to consider social changes, crises, and developments, as well as more static situations. Rein Raud, for example, not only entitles his book as *Asian Worldviews* but gives as its subtitle, 'Religions, Philosophies, Political Theories', making it perfectly clear how those three domains interplay within many Asian contexts, not least that of China (2021). Much the same could be said for the emergence of many forms of Christianity that rose out of Judaism, spread throughout Europe and then across the world through military imperial conquests, commercialism, and evangelism.

To take only one example, divisions in Christianity often prompted new narratives of the Bible catalysed by politics and established religion as with the Protestant Pilgrim Fathers, dissenting from England's formal state religion and establishing an American colony in 1620. Their favoured biblical motif of a city on a hill became a later US self-image as a beacon of democracy for the whole world (Matthew 5:14). By contrast, the late eighteenth-century French Revolution sought an end to Monarchy and its intrinsic sense of divine right of kings, despite the military hero Napoleon Bonaparte's coronation (1804) that ultimately led to a Republic separating church and state and fostering the notion of *laïcité*, established by law in 1905, to distinguish between the secular state and religious involvements. That complex worldview, for example, now poses issues with Muslim citizens in the early twenty-first century over religious dress in public places and institutions. Another extensive ideological transformation emerged as Russia developed into the Union of Soviet Socialist Republics in the 1920s and endured until 1991. Then, from the second decade of the twenty-first century, Orthodox Religion regained a position in public life, often in a degree of co-operation with Russian political agents.

From the late eighteenth century until present times, various Protestant European States, notably the Dutch, French, German, and British, established Empires across the world, not least in different parts of Africa. These benefitted economically while also engaging in missionary activity of their own denominational forms of Christianity, much as Catholic Spain and Portugal had previously done in South America (Yates, 2004). One aspect of European power and colonisation that sustained the growing workforce on plantations in America's southern states and in the West Indies concerned forced slavery, with multitudes of black Africans being shipped across the Atlantic at notable cost to their health, loss, and enduring racial disadvantage in the USA. Christian theology and associated church alliance with state powers sustained this, and something similar underlay the notion of *Apartheid* in South Africa. While some Christian leaders came to object to these practices, deep racial problems endure. The Black Lives Matter protests of 2021, originating in the USA with the abusive treatment of black citizens, usually by white police, show ongoing forms of worldview that find resonance in wider cultural commitments to the rule of law, human rights, and the value of individuals.

So, too, with the twentieth century's Great War in Europe between 1914 and 1918, and the Second World War of 1939–1945 whose Nazi force in Germany revealed virulent ant-Semitism, with the Third Reich's desire for an empire of pure-blooded people that would last a thousand years: it ended in 1945. The post-war division of Berlin between the victorious USA, UK, and USSR allies soon led to the 'Cold-War' (1947–1991) between the Soviet Union and western Democratic Nations and marked a new worldview-style division of political regimes. Another political upheaval, the rise of the People's Republic of China (from 1949) marked the development of its still-growing worldview rooted in a distinctive, centralised, socialist ideology. This included the transformation of Tibet, whose own form of Theocracy embodied in the Dalai Lama constituted something of its own worldview. His migration to India in 1959 left the land under the rule of the People's Republic of China.

The Second World War transformed the world on an even grander scale through the scientific-engineering work generating the atomic bomb and its devastating use by the USA on the Japanese cities of Hiroshima and Nagasaki in August 1945. The subsequent atomic arms race, and the Cold War between the USSR and the USA and their respective allies from around the late 1940s to 1990s marked the twentieth century in ideological terms, some seeing the peril of atomic and nuclear warfare as having restrained ultimate mutual destruction, even though limited conventional warfare continued in many world contexts. To speak of an atomic-nuclear worldview is to highlight the complexity of the 'worldview' topic, one affecting high-level political regimes but probably not affecting ordinary attitudes. However, the Cuba Missile Crisis of 1962, involving a stand-off between the USSR and the USA, raised just such concerns, not least amongst teenage generations born into a relatively 'safe' world after 1945 but now emotionally alerted to international political dangers with countries able to devastate the civilised world.

Conclusion

These historical cases prompt debate and dispute, whether over political power or, in quite a different fashion, over the intellectual force of, for example, the big-picture of evolutionary development of the later nineteenth century. Just as some Christians adopted versions of evolution with, potentially, some divine influence, others advocate a 'Creationist' view reckoned to be more directly expressive of biblical ideas. Such historical notes are reminders of how societies are influenced by their own history and contemporary reflection, and of how they can be imposed on others, something that remains true for ideas of worldview and for 'religion' itself, as the next two chapters show.

1 Framing worldviews

Introduction

This chapter's brief account of how the worldview idea has occurred in the study of religion highlights key theoretical issues surrounding the cultural dominance of western philosophical theorising, the way 'worldview' has been used to bolster one major psychological innovation, and the perennial issue of the relationship between social groups and their members captured in the idiom of 'individual-society'. It also introduces the idea of ethnography as a 'worldview' study.

Philosophy, sociology, and social worlds

In terms of background history, Wilhelm Dilthey (1833–1911) developed a philosophical approach to human groups, their worldviews, and the scholarly need to 'understand' people through the very fact of being human ourselves. A late essay (Dilthey, 1911) offered a triple classification of worldviews typified as 'naturalism', 'idealism of freedom', and 'objective idealism'. His concern to develop a scholarly approach to social science as the expression of the human 'spirit' (*Geisteswissenschaft*) is often captured in Max Weber's idea of *verstehen* or the 'understanding' one thinker may intuit of other people's circumstances.

Weber (1864–1920) focused on the sociological interplay of practical, ethical, and economic behaviour underlying different societies, captured in their distinctive 'orientations to the world' – his version of 'worldview – rooted in a 'basic "drive" towards meaning' that, in terms of this study, easily takes the form of 'the *need for salvation*' (Parsons, 1966:xxxii, xlvii, xlix). Weber's abstract analysis of a group's 'orientation to the world' stands as a clear theoretical notion and is less likely to be found in everyday conversation unlike 'worldview' that easily carries an ordinary usage. This is a reminder that some terms have both ordinary and technical-scholarly

DOI: 10.4324/9781003242437-3

significance. Parsons detects in Weber's work – and this would include his orientation to the world – an 'emphasis on *differentiation*' that approaches key issues through some binary distinction, one focusing on change and the other on maintaining the existing order of things. One example would be interpreting the need for salvation with either 'asceticism' or 'mysticism' as its practical response (Parsons, 1966:xxix, li). More broadly speaking Weber's sociology of religion encompasses a series of orientations to the world embracing diverse contexts, occupations, and social classes, from shopkeepers to soldiers: these and others follow 'different roads to salvation' (Weber, 1964:151–65). Weber used the technical idea of an ideal type to capture and compare key features of religious traditions, such as prophets and capitalists, and also ideas of religious ethics as a combination of emotional and ideological aspects of life, as discussed later between ordinary and technical usage of 'worldview' as these will arise throughout this book.

Psychology and Freud's 'Question of a Weltanschauung'

Unlike Weber's social dynamics and orientation to the world, Sigmund Freud (1856–1939) focused on the dynamics of conscious and unconscious awareness. He sought to establish psychoanalysis as its own scientific activity and worldview. Influentially straddling the nineteenth and twentieth centuries, Freud abandoned biology to develop his own theory and practice of Psychoanalysis to explore human behaviour through its conscious and unconscious mental processes, shepherding the world of dreams, phantasies, and wish-fulfilment into a thought-world of its own. His critical accounts of religion, especially of Christianity as derived from Judaism, emphasised human wish-fulfilment and desire to trust in an ultimate Deity who could be relied upon when earthly parents failed and died. Although his studies of *Totem and Taboo* (1912), *The Future of an Illusion* (1927), and *Moses and Monotheism* (1934) are nearly always cited in Religious Studies, one seldom-cited paper concerns 'The Question of a Weltanschauung'. Originally given as a lecture, it answered 'a question that is constantly being asked – does psychoanalysis lead to a particular *Weltanschauung*, and if so, to which?' (Freud, 1973:193). Here Freud prompts a new way of looking at life, poses key existential questions, and decides to keep the German word while alert to problems of definition and translation into other languages. He speaks of *Weltanschauung* as an,

> intellectual construction which solves all the problems of our existence uniformly on the basis of one overriding hypothesis, which, accordingly, leaves no question unanswered and in which everything that interests us finds its fixed place.
>
> (Freud, 1973:193)

For Freud, psychoanalysis was a sub-set of a scientific worldview superseding the interpretations of existence offered by religion. He speaks of 'the struggle of the scientific spirit against the religious *Weltanschauung*' as being 'as you know, not at an end: it is still going on under our eyes' (Freud, 1973:203). For him, science improved on religion for three reasons. First, religion answers a desire for knowledge about the meaning of the world, which brings religion into competition with science. Second, religion offers comfort and security against danger. Even though some are abandoned to pain or distress, science is deemed less helpful. Third, religion lays down laws and rules by which to live, and while science may also arrive at helpful rules for life, it does so through its empirical work and not on the basis of 'revelation, intuition, or divination' (Freud, 1973:194–97). In his lecture, Freud touches on two potentially competitive worldviews. First, that kind of philosophical anarchy in which, 'there is no such thing as truth', a position that resonates with what decades later would concern cultural relativity and post-modern deconstruction. The second focused on Marxism, then establishing itself as a political-state organisation in Russia, and leaving him wondering about its future (Freud, 1973:213–18). Overall, Freud saw psychoanalysis as a branch of psychology that brought both the 'intellectual and emotional function of men (and of animals)' into science as such (Freud, 1973:194). His emphasis on the idea of *Weltanschauung*, provides valuable early insight into the very idea of a worldview as an explanatory scheme of things.

Worldviews, power, and domination

Freud's psychoanalytic domain gained enormous twentieth-century significance. Though now existing in some flourishing yet restricted psychiatric, literary, and philosophical circles, many scientifically minded psychiatrists and psychologists seriously doubt its premises. As for Weber and many sociologists, their concerns with the dynamics of individuals in society only developed further, while from the later twenty-first-century critiques of colonial and postcolonial contexts merit brief mention here, while issues of sex-gender and identity are taken up in a later worldview. Of many scholars of power and postcolonialism, three are sketched here: Keane is largely oblivious to colonial-imperialist issues, Haddon begins to mark its problems, and Said famously explores them.

Keane, colonial-imperialism

A. H. Keane (1833–1912) exemplifies an entrenched colonialism now regarded as western and patronising. Involved with various anthropological societies, he published much, including *The World's Peoples Popular Account of Their Bodily and Mental Characters, Beliefs, Traditions, Political and Social Institutions* (1908). It was a compendium of attitudes to life without using the word 'worldview', all grounded in notions of ethnic origin. The 'Sterling qualities of the English race' provide a hallmark for a people who are 'in several respects the dominant people amongst both civilized and uncivilized races': he lists British colonial territories and the English language dominance in the USA. Indeed, 'it is easily seen that, humanly speaking, the future destinies of mankind must be largely controlled by the peoples of English speech', characterised by their 'intense love of freedom and independence combined with an almost cold-blooded indifference to risks and danger' and who have 'created the finest literature in the world' as well as numerous, and named, scientists (1908:378–81). Apart from a sentence on Puritans and 'odious Calvinistic teachings', he largely avoids religious topics for England, but most other peoples, their religion, or magic, are often depicted with superlative negativity. It is difficult, for example, to get a 'Welshman to look facts straight in the face'; he is 'either dreaming of past glories ... or ready to fall into hysterics at the next revivalist meeting', with 'the whole nation rejecting the Episcopalian doctrines of the English Church and are nearly all dissenters, Baptists, and Calvinists'; still, he admits of some excellence in poetry and music (1908:348). Meanwhile, the Tibetans are 'certainly the victims of a depressing priestly rule, a vast organised system of hypocrisy, with a veneer of Buddhism above the old pagan beliefs', including a 'most pernicious veneer of Lamaism or grasping priestcraft', accordingly, 'religion itself is mainly a system of magic, the sole aim of worship being to baffle the machinations of the demons' (1908:189–90). So continues his descriptive interpretation of the world's peoples.

A. C. Haddon

Unlike Keane, Alfred C. Haddon (1855–1940), Reader in Ethnology at Cambridge, published a judicious and early *History of Anthropology* (1910). From the classical antiquity of Hippocrates and Aristotle, through contemporary European social thought, and the contributions of psychology, linguistics, archaeology, geography and environment, it includes a chapter 'Sociology and Religion'. Though brief, Haddon remains valuable for at least two points concerning worldviews, one on conceptual shifts, another on ethics.

First, he describes contemporary science-like attitudes on society as divided between the 'classic, orthodox, catastrophic, or creationist party' on the one hand and the 'evolutionists or transmutationists' on the other (1910:62). While (pre-Darwinian) evolutionists rejected special divine creation and held to 'some unknown law', it was 1859 and Darwin's work on natural selection that transformed public opinion by providing a rationale. Haddon cites Alfred Russell Wallace on 'this vast, this totally unprecedented, change in public opinion ... brought about in the short space of twenty years' (1910:63).

Here, in effect, we witness a worldview and conceptual paradigm shift of the highest level, much as in a later chapter, we see something similar in the emergence of Gaia theory of world self-regulation (Lovelock, 1979).

Second, Haddon sketches the 'ferment' prompted by Darwin's scheme, notes critiques and developments of it, but rapidly brings the discussion to 'different races', their diversity or similarity of intelligence, and to slavery. Haddon's impartiality is much tested when decrying one publication on 'racial' differences as a 'preposterous book' that could appeal only 'to the ignorant and bigoted (1910:68). That book's title, by Charles Carroll, would now offend many and is practically unprintable today. Observing anthropology as a young discipline with a 'fascination and popularity' that 'tend to premature generalizations ... prejudice and bigotry', Haddon thought that 'reactionaries have always had to give way in the end, especially as 'intensive studies of limited areas' overtake simplistic generalisation (1910:154).

Edward Said, orientalism and occidental bias

Born in Jerusalem, educated in Egypt and prime American Universities, Edward Said (1935–2003) was a literary scholar with work embracing political, religious, and cultural analyses of Mediterranean societies. His influential book *Orientalism* covers those themes while exploring western scholars' detailed linguistic and historical studies of places such as Lebanon, Palestine, Israel, and Egypt. However, these were often driven by 'their feelings of superiority about European culture, even as their antipathy spread to include the entire Orient, of which Islam was considered a degraded (and usually, a virulently dangerous) representative'; they were also probably influenced by nineteenth-century western ideas influenced by the Bible ([1978] 2003:260). For him, Orientalism was a 'system of ideological fictions' that emerged as a western construct of its own, and which is essentially 'intellectually discreditable'; he did not think it was a simple product of the 'insider-outsider' argument derived from the American sociologist Robert Merton; as for Max Weber's use of 'types' such as 'Oriental, Islamic, Arab or whatever', Said found them inadequate ([1978] 2003:321–2, 260). In effect, *Orientalism* provides its own kind of worldview study that depicts, analyses, and critiques generations of western scholars and their construction of an oriental worldview. Said expresses ethical concerns over the USA's interest in the politics and economics of the Near-Eastern countries, and a certain scholarly shame of experts advising the American government on the basis of an orientalist perspective. However, he exempts anthropologist Clifford Geertz whose 'interest in Islam is discrete and concrete enough to be animated by the specific societies and problems he studies and not by the ritual, preconceptions, and doctrines of Orientalism' ([1978] 2003:326).

Ninian Smart dimensions and worldviews

An approximate age-mate of Said, Smart (1927–2001) offered a different venture in worldview studies. This Scot influenced the very notion of Religious Studies in the English-speaking world through books, graduate students, an international scholarly presence, and in the formation of a distinctive Department of Religious Studies at Lancaster University from the mid twentieth to early twenty-first century. His *Worldviews: Crosscultural Explorations of Human Beliefs* (1995) provides an introduction to the study of religion through a focus on 'dimensions of religion', developed further in *Dimensions of the Sacred* (1996) as doctrinal and philosophical, mythical and narrative, ethical or legal, ritual or practical, experiential or emotional, social or institutional dimensions ([1995] 2000:8–10). *Dimensions* is important for pursuing a comparative study of religion alongside a recognition of secular ideologies, and for linking these as ways in which people 'interact thoughtfully with the cosmos and express the exigencies of our nature and existence', making his study 'a kind of physiology of spirituality and of worldviews', or 'a version of worldview analysis', approached as an 'incarnated worldview' (1996:1–2). He did not want to overplay abstract beliefs and doctrines and ignore how they are practically rooted and, today, his intentions would probably be expressed in terms of embodiment and lived experience. He offered a sevenfold 'dimensional analysis of worldviews' typified as (i) ritual or practical, (ii) doctrinal or philosophical, (iii) mythic or narrative, (iv) experiential or emotional, (v) ethical or legal, (vi) organisational or social, and (vii) material or artistic (1996:8–11). He provided a religious sketch-analysis of mainstream Christianity and of USA Nationalism, one religious, the other secular, and also mapped links between these dimensions and established academic disciplines. The rest of his book covers major world religions and ideologies through his seven dimensions.

Ethnography as worldviews?

The method that best meets Smart's desire not to ignore the embodied life-contexts of people is ethnography – a foundational method in anthropology, and important for worldview studies since each ethnography tends to generate the worldview of a people. From the evolution-inspired yet speculative phase of the 1870s, anthropology rapidly developed in the twentieth century through its chosen method of 'ethnography', a term that combines the familiar idea of fieldwork, participant-observation, writing up accounts and presenting a formal analysis of it. Fieldwork usually focused upon a single community's linguistic and networked relationships that frame its way of life, its basis of survival and cultural flourishing. Through this process, the ethnographer documents, photographs, records, and films materials that bring the lives of others into our own purview. Recent evolutionary and cognitive anthropology has brought other perspectives to bear as we see later. Ethnographies often encounter Worldview Studies through the process of comparison. Though here some care is needed because 'comparative religion' and 'world religions' were common in late-nineteenth and early twentieth-century study of religion, often focused on sacred scriptures, doctrines, and histories. 'Religious studies' came into favour in the later twentieth and early twenty-first centuries and opened up such 'library' studies to a variety of social scientific methods and theories. Functionalist models considered how social institutions met basic human and emotional needs (Malinowski, ([1948] 1974), others focused on how the brain works in shaping human thought and behaviour (Sperber, 1975), yet others stress how the material environment and human labour mould societies. With the closing decades of the twentieth century and the opening years of the new century, critical voices pinpointed colonial, postcolonial, gendered, and autobiographical dynamics that influence anthropological analysis, with issues of power and identity streaming through self-analysis and disciplinary doubt associated with the privileged 'western' desire to study 'others'. These debates continue in newer perspectives on studies of one's 'own' society (Miller, 2008, 2010) or in the use of cognitive psychology and evolutionary anthropology (Boyer, 1993).

Lienhardt's Dinka

Despite furnishing extensive data that frame and fill a group's view of the world, most ethnographic studies seldom speak of worldviews. While many ethnographies could exemplify this, Godfrey Lienhardt's account of the Dinka of the Sudan offers a fine example. Entitled *Divinity and Experience* (1961) this magisterial work takes the reader into Dinka experiences of life and the forces perceived to impinge upon existence. It depicts context-linked behaviours that prompt expressions and actions that many readers would see as religious.

Within the single world known to them (for they dwell little upon fancies of any 'other world' of different constitutions) the Dinka claim that they encounter 'spirits' of various kinds, which they call generically *jok*. In this account I call them 'Powers'.

(1961:28)

With the term 'Powers', he begins a process of interpretation while remaining vigilant over making comparisons and contrasts of ideas, beliefs, and potential theological similarities, so as not to disregard Dinka complexity or to draw too easy a parallel between 'them' and 'us'. Where 'we' are westerners with a Christian cultural heritage. Lienhardt draws heavily from Dinka myths and ethnographic detail when presenting a sociological form of analysis showing how myths of origin tell of a close unity of Powers and people until human actions lead to a division of things into a 'radically divided world' (1961:32). The issue of mortality and the desire for life to triumph over death is captured in the burial alive of the Master of the Fishing Spear. He dies voluntarily and for the people and is not overcome by death. To read Lienhardt's ethnography is to gain some sense of a Dinka worldview, presented in context and indigenous terms, but also with an analytical interpretation. As such it is a good example of what is often called an 'etic' view, namely an interpretation made by the researcher, as opposed to 'emic' explanations offered by the people studied when they reflect upon what they do and say, a valuable distinction for worldview studies.

Droogers and van Harskamp

A generation after Lienhardt's interlinked combination of description and interpretation, and deeply influenced by ethnographic practice, André Droogers and Anton van Harskamp produced a significant edited volume that explicitly differentiated between description and interpretation in their *Methods for the Study of Religious Change: From Religious Studies to Worldview Studies* (2014). This emphasises a theoretical direction of flow 'from' Religious Studies 'to' Worldview Studies while providing a series of case studies conducted in Holland. Their influential volume explicitly follows the 'meaning-making' pathway, intentionally locating 'religion as a sub-category of the term worldview' and highlighting both the potential difficulties and benefits of 'experiencing the emotional and physical sensations that often accompany ritual' while also welcoming interdisciplinary approaches (2014:2,11). In both practical and theoretical terms, their work is pivotal for setting a worldview agenda for the study of religious movements and has stimulated this present study: we return to it when discussing the Ludic Worldview. Their 'meaning-making' approach echoes aspects of my own previous work on anthropological hermeneutics, the sociology of knowledge, and Religious Studies (Davies, 1984).

UK religious education

One important issue for worldview studies in the British context occurred when the Religious Education Council of England and Wales published a report of the Commission on Religious Education (CORE) entitled *Religion and Worldviews: The Way Forward: A National Plan for Religious Education* (2018). Explicitly using the notion of *Weltanshauung* (German – worldview), it differentiates between 'institutional worldviews' as 'organised worldviews' that are 'sometimes embedded in institutions', and 'personal worldviews for an individual's own way of understanding and living in the world, which may or may not draw from one, or many, institutional worldviews' (2018:4). It is, partly at least, to the question-raising nature of that Report that this present book responds.

Individual–society

This relationship between institutional and personal worldviews is highly significant, having long been the prime issue in sociology and philosophy. Here and in later chapters, this interplay is captured in the notion of identity, probably the most important and all-pervading concept that straddles issues in the study of religion, as it does across many issues in social science, the arts, and humanities. It also appears in the complex world of medicine and how a single person's DNA, health, and wellbeing relate to their environmental and social contexts. This is a reminder of how anthropology, sociology, psychology, history, and the study of religion all depend on the focus and level of description and analysis and of how they can relate to each other. And this is why methodology – as the study of different methods and their appropriateness for specific tasks – is a vital aspect in the study of phenomena often described as 'religious'.

The difference between national census data gained through questionnaires and the more immediate information gathered from fieldwork engagement with a group can be enormous. While much formal attention is often paid to the former as quantitative and the latter as qualitative research, in practice much is gained by relating them. The best kind of academic work often integrates historical, archival material to frame statistical evidence or to contextualise the psychologist's case study of a single person. The researcher's own life, religious, secular, or mixed experiences are also important and place considerable demands upon people, given the need for a grasp of the range of methods, as well as the responsibility surrounding ethical aspects of research. This has long been true in theology where historical, textual, philosophical, and social-contextual forms of analysis have been incorporated into interpretations of religious beliefs and practices. Similarly, social–cultural anthropology has been influenced by evolutionary, linguistic, and psychological ideas, as well as by the importance of personal biography and a reflexive approach to working with and amongst different groups, so too with studies of literature, history, philosophy, and art. The early twenty-first century has also brought cognitive psychology, evolutionary anthropology, and ecological–environmental studies to the fore. Not forgetting issues of power and control that dominate political, colonial, sex-gender, ethnic-origin, and environmental topics, all of which underlie identity-based issues many of which emerge in subsequent chapters. For the moment, however, the pressing topic of personal prejudice and orientation needs consideration.

'Sider-ness', prejudice, and knowledge

Personal prejudices, loves, and hostilities are often embedded in a scholar's personal experiences of religious traditions and distinctive worldviews, and it is wise for academics to be as alert to these as is psychologically possible. Some are born into a religious tradition and increasingly appropriate it to their personal and social advantage. In England, for example, someone brought up in the Church of England can find an easy congruence between their ecclesial identity and other institutional aspects of cultural life. They accumulate cultural capital from a shared sense of belonging and values, and even if they abandon formal religiosity, they often retain its ethos in their choice of profession (Davies and Guest, 2007). In Britain, theology is an academic study pursued by numerous scholars embedded within high-status religious institutions and with extensive social capital. Some high-status universities sustain professorial positions shared with Church of England appointments as Canon Professors, as well as formal College Chaplaincies, something similar obtains in hospitals and prisons, as well as in many Public Schools whose chaplains, chapels, and pastoral care provide their own influential, if low-key, presence. So, too, in state schools having religious patronage. Sometimes these institutional factors influence people's preferences for retaining the idea of Religious Education and Religious Studies rather than adopting a Worldviews perspective.

A different scenario involves those who reject their own religious background but find a satisfying alternative in the study of religion or in some professional work, a topic revealing both the dynamic possibilities of change within a person's identity and how some deeply embodied beliefs are perpetuated through a process of 'transformed retention' (Davies and

Northam-Jones, 2012). Indeed, the very study of religion can become its own kind of life-commitment that overtakes previous faith-commitments. For some, a long-term socialisation in a religious group engenders a way of speaking about life as an insider, and their switch to an 'outsider' status as far as personal conviction is concerned is ameliorated by talking about religion rather than testifying to it on a conviction base. Some who leave sectarian groups of close-knit relationships, for example, can find life extremely difficult, and explain the existence of mutual support groups of 'leavers'. These still spend much time talking about those traditions albeit from a different perspective. It may well be that even negative criticism of a group still satisfies an engagement with its grammar of discourse. There is, in fact, a growing field of research on 'leaving religion' (Enstedt et al., 2020). Recent decades have often foregrounded autobiographical factors and even theorised them in notions of reflexivity as well as in the notion of an insider-outsider status in relation to religious groups. This last concept should, however, be treated with great care since there are many degrees of insider-ness / outsider-ness associated with different contexts, issues, groups, and stages of life.

Worldviews, social class, belonging

Issues of belonging, change, and identity often involve social class, professionalism, educational qualification, and political–cultural allegiance. One intriguing example touches on what might be called cultural worldviews in British political life as imaginatively depicted by David Goodhart. In his 'binary distinction between Anywhere and Somewhere worldviews … and values', he constructs an ideal-type differentiation of 'value clusters'. Liberal elites, largely middle-class, centred upon London's political networks see the wide world as their potential sphere of operation; by contrast, largely working-class people hold a strong sense of locality and identity; hence his 'Anywhere' and 'Somewhere' ideal-types (Goodhart, 2017:23). That discussion of worldview issues is not concerned with religion but with wider social values prompted by the majority British view to exit the European Union that shocked the political elites. He was also concerned with populist revolts more generally, especially the election of Donald Trump as American president. These issues are also deeply linked to emotions, values, and identity that will be explored in the next chapter.

One similar approach to social class is Richard Hoggart's influential work on British society. He, too, is insightfully alert to loose elements that can cohere in a telling cluster of ideas. In one paragraph, he lists a dozen or more popular sayings that, together, advocate 'Tolerance, belonging and charity', while another three pages cite verses from hymns that he reckoned even 'a long-time agnostic' – presumably himself – could find in 'an always present, even if fractured, moral frame' (Hoggart, 1995:276,273, respectively). Goodhart's 'value clusters' and Hoggart's 'moral frame' mark issues informing a person's identity. A different approach to identity and supernatural figures has been long-pursued in psychological theories, including attachment theory. Though the latter has often been used to discuss both child development and the dynamic nature of bereavement and grief (Davies, 2017:53–78), it has more recently been taken into analyses of religion and various forms of attachment to God (Granqvist, 2020), discussed in a later chapter.

Conclusion

Worldviews, then, can be understood at implicit and explicit levels of discussion in relation to processes of meaning-making, attachment, and orientation to the world. One advantage of this approach lies in coping with terms such as religion, spirituality, secularity, and ideology, and with Religious Studies itself. This is highly significant for education at school, college, and university levels and for policy decision-making, because it contrasts differing, contradictory, and interest-driven concerns, as the next chapter shows.

2   Religion and religious studies

Introduction

This chapter's concern with definitions recognises that they are not only important for giving a clear direction of study but also problematic and divisive, especially with the concept of 'religion' that divides those who are assured that divine entities exist in their own right and those for whom they are purely human constructs. This has consequences both for the notion of Religious Studies and for Worldview Studies, with additional significance for issues of identity and the place of emotion in undergirding people's standpoints.

Categories

At its most basic, some take 'religion' as a domain of experience that cannot be explained by some other approach, especially psychology or economics. They speak of something that is *sui generis,* a Latin phrase asserting a self-generated property, something born of itself and demanding its own tailor-made method of study. Others, taking 'religion' to be the outcome of human creativity, adopt wider cultural, political, economic, psychological, and aesthetic approaches; they sometimes criticise 'religion' as an essentially western category that is too easily and misleadingly imposed on Eastern traditions and human behaviour at large. They see the *sui generis* case as reification, or establishing something as being far more certain than it is. Because this process of classification is often influenced by a scholar's sense of identity, the issue of identity-theory will occupy part of this chapter.

Often, however, arguments are less polarised and depend upon the power of particular theories in accounting for the complexity of the world and of personal experience, and sometimes theories simply rise and fall in significance as a kind of intellectual fashion. Currently, theories of Durkheim, Weber, Freud, Otto, Cantwell Smith, and Geertz are all well-known, as is

DOI: 10.4324/9781003242437-4

that of Fitzgerald and some others who establish their concerns over using 'religion' at all. By contrast Hans Mol is seldom cited in the study of religion despite his powerful theory of the sacralisation of identity. Today, cognitive studies has already established its position (Boyer, 1993), whereas Granqvist (2020) and his development of attachment theory for religion is only just making its presence felt, despite attachment theory having been long-familiar in psychological studies of grief.

Religion, western idea, export, and imposition

Timothy Fitzgerald is one representative scholar who seriously opposes the terms 'religion' and 'Religious Studies'. For him, there is nothing 'beyond the fundamental values, conceptions, and social relations of specific societies', and no supernaturally divine cluster of entities exists (2000:245). Following notions of projection notably argued by Feuerbach and Freud, human feelings and desires are projected upon imagined supernatural entities that are subsequently sensed as real and are appropriated as such by ongoing generations. Durkheim saw 'religious force' as 'only the sentiment inspired by the group in its members, but projected outside of the consciousnesses that experience them, and objectified', and it is when this is 'superimposed' upon something that it becomes 'sacred' (Durkheim, [1915] 1971:228–9). Despite criticism over speculative interpretations of Australian Aboriginal materials and the way 'western' Judaeo-Christian traditions pervaded his cultural heritage, as had France's secular revolution, Durkheim's *Elementary Forms of the Religious Life* remains an inspiring masterpiece ([1915] 1971).

Fitzgerald follows this projectionist approach. Transcendence is not some state of experience of God, but an experience generated by devotees themselves much as Durkheim proposed. For Fitzgerald, however, it also becomes a philosophical and existential thrust against theological assumptions that supernatural agents lie behind 'religion'. He is concerned that influences associated with religion as a faith-position implicitly pervade academic contexts, granting 'Religious Studies', or indeed the 'Anthropology of Religion', an unmerited authenticity. He is, for example, critical of the anthropologist Maurice Bloch for using 'religion' in a loose way while commending Bloch's theory of rebounding violence or rebounding conquest as a human-rooted process that replaces the natural facts of life and death with new, cultural 'facts of life'. In other words, an anthropologist who normally 'rejects religion as an analytical category' ought not to let that category slip into his discussion of what is, essentially, an account of 'culture understood as ritual process, values, construction of transcendental identity, and the legitimation of power' (Fitzgerald, 2000:248–9). Still, he applauds Bloch's interest in ritual processes that change how people feel and think about themselves.

Interestingly both Durkheim and Freud, in their shared secular Jewish contexts, found inspiration for their respective theories of projection and transcendence in the work of Scottish Protestant theologian and Arabic scholar, William Robertson Smith (1846–1894). His *Religion of the Semites* (1894) depicted a 'communion theory' of sacrifice in which human devotees and supernatural sources shared together in a joyous ceremony that left devotees exalted and stronger than they were before. Here lay the prompting resource for Freud's notion of primal patricide and Durkheim's collective rites that foster a sense of transcendence, albeit by excluding Smith's personal Christian sense of divine reality.

God is God

It is over transcendence that this issue becomes clearest as devotees testify to sensing a supernatural dimension of life involving an encounter with God, spirits, ancestors, or otherwise 'dead' relatives. Such experiences provide their own proof and encourage studies of what might be called comparative transcendence, and have certainly fostered the more familiar idea of Comparative Religion. The German philosopher, theologian, and historian of religions Rudolph Otto (1869–1937) exemplified this in his account of 'the idea of the Holy' depicted as a forcefully attractive and awe-inspiring mystery a *mysterium tremendum et fascinans*, as he described it in Latin; something that can be accessed through a 'mental state' that is 'perfectly *sui generis* and irreducible to any other' (1924:7). This echoes Friedrich Schleiermacher's approach to religion grounded in what today would be called 'lived experience'. For him, 'the true nature of religion' lies in an 'immediate consciousness of the Deity as He is found in ourselves and in the world'. This includes an 'immortality which we can have now in this temporal life', granting the devotee, 'in the midst of finitude to be one with the Infinite', and in every moment to be eternal', this 'is the immortality of religion' (Schleiermacher, 1958:101). Otto's introduction to one of Schleiermacher's studies sees it as a commentary on 'the disappearing or already vanished ... world views of the "Enlightenment" ... with its autonomous culture and morality', or we might say its own worldview (Schleiermacher, 1958:xi).

Religion: definitions and descriptions

This distinction between religion as real in itself or as an imaginative human creation is enormously significant. At its sharpest, it expresses the distinction between God being there or not, something of deep concern to many people's grasp of life, and central to many faith-based theological studies. Social scientific accounts of human existence largely view ideas of God as social constructs – God is not 'there', exemplified in Durkheim's and Geertz's early and later twentieth-century definitions that have attracted much reference, acceptance, and criticism.

Emile Durkheim (1858–1917) and Clifford Geertz (1926–2006)

Durkheim's quintessential sociological approach proposes:

> Religion is a unified system of beliefs and practices relative to sacred things, that is to say, things set apart and forbidden – beliefs and practices which unite into one single moral community called a Church, all those who adhere to them.
>
> ([1915] 1971:47)

Geertz's anthropological approach, often identified as a 'cultural definition', proposes:

> Religion is a system of symbols which acts to establish powerful, pervasive and long-lasting moods and motivations in men by formulating conceptions of a general order of existence and clothing those conceptions with such an aura of factuality that these moods and motivations seem uniquely realistic.
>
> (1993:90)

Both speak of a 'system'; Durkheim's unifies beliefs and practices around sacred phenomena which are, essentially, ritual-symbols that foster community integration by intensifying experience and evoking a sense of something greater than themselves. Durkheim identifies this as nothing less than 'society' itself even though participants regard the experience as ancestral or divine presence. He equates God and society. Durkheim's 'beliefs' can be equated with Geertz's 'conceptions of a general order of existence', and his 'practices' with Geertz's 'system of symbols' found in ritual and wider aspects of cultural life. Geertz brings emotions into greater play in his system of symbols and this is a crucial development, for Durkheim subordinates emotion to social factors because he wanted to establish sociology as a distinctive method over psychology by highlighting 'social facts' rather than psychological states. Geertz pinpointed 'moods and motivations' to stress symbolic aspects of cultural life. His phrase is remarkably similar to the issue of 'mood' discussed further for Weber who preceded Geertz.

Geertz's pre-occupation with moods is important not just for his cultural definition of religion but also for our interest in seeking a definition of worldviews. For, in an early essay, he linked both of these.

A people's ethos is the tone, character, and quality of their life, its moral and aesthetic style and mood: it is the underlying attitude towards themselves and their world that life reflects. Their worldview is the picture of the way things, in sheer actuality are, their concept of nature, of self, of society.

(1957:421)

To this we return in our final chapter, but here it highlights the anthropological use of 'worldview' in the 1950s alongside a cluster of emotion-linked terms – ethos, tone, quality, mood, and aesthetic style. To this dynamic account of the 'feel' of a situation, Geertz adds a picturing of life and the more abstract 'concept of nature ... self ... society'. This 'picturing' element recurs in the notion of paradigmatic scenes in chapter four, as well as elsewhere in the notion of an ideal type or summarising basic elements of a situation.

Gregory Bateson (1904–1980)

Before Geertz, Bateson's seminal account of the *Iatmul* people of New Guinea had discussed the emotional 'tones indicative of an ethos', and the 'expressions of a standardized system of emotional values', leading him to consider the 'organization of the instincts and emotions of the individuals' of a society (Bateson [1935] 1958:118–19). Just how societies foster a particular ethos and how individuals accept or reject them remains an ongoing issue for worldview studies, but Bateson provided major signposts for this work, including analysis of communication theories and ways of understanding mental illness. He developed the idea of deutero-learning, already used in chapter one, and his widespread anthropological and psychological interests made him deeply aware of what he called a 'confusion of spheres of relevance', which easily arises if we confuse 'our study of the psychological processes of the individual with our study of society as a whole' ([1935] 1958:176). Being alert to the different 'spheres of relevance' remains important for Worldview Religious Studies when considering the relationship between society at large and its individual members. Bateson's hope that future studies might develop this whole field of ethos and tones of different groups has not, as yet, emerged within Religious Studies, let alone Worldview Studies, though some suggestions will be made in Part Two of this study.

Max Weber *(1864–1920)*

Returning to definitions we find Weber's essay on 'The Rise of Religions' arguing that,

> to define 'religion', to say what it is, is not possible at the start of a presentation such as this. Definition can be attempted, if at all, only at the conclusion of the study. The essence of religion is not even our concern, as we make it our task to study the conditions and effects of a particular type of social behaviour.
>
> ([1922] 1966:1)

In effect, Weber avoids a sharply propositional definition of religion, preferring his ideal-type descriptions of 'extraordinary powers' noted by devotees. He speaks in general terms of 'religious' as of 'magical behaviour', and adopts the notion of 'charisma' to embrace both, while never forgetting wider aspects of life, including economics and political power ([1922] 1966:1–3). Social complexity, and the need to identify mutually influencing forces, underlie Weber's approach to what many narrowly define as 'religion', and one key contribution concerns what is often translated as 'mood', and which aligns with what has already been said for Geertz and Bateson.

This is found in Weber's German concept of *gesinnungsethik* that brings together thought and emotion in an 'ethic of moral sentiment' (Parsons, 1966:lv). It links abstraction with feeling to create a mood affecting a devotee's life orientation. This is a valuable concept for understanding how ideology or doctrinal materials engage with the emotional dynamics of a person or group. The best-known example concerns his Protestant Ethic argument that correlated the theological idea of Predestination – that God allocated people to being saved or damned just as He willed, with the believer's practical lifestyle. They accept that they can never know just who is on the saved or damned list because God's will is inscrutable, but they find that if they live according to divine edicts, their scrupulous behaviour generates success, allowing them to invoke the idea that God blesses his chosen ones. So they identify with the saved by a kind of indirect theological logic. Psychologically, this gives a sense of relief from the potential dissonance of not knowing their ultimate status. Weber depicts other forms of devotional, ritual, and mystical life, leading to the assertion that 'the religious mood is the true instrument of salvation', suggesting that mystical truths may 'assume a central position within, and ... exert an integrating influence upon, the total view of the world' ([1922] 1966:151, 171).

Meaning and sensing

Just as Weber's use of 'mood' as part of people's drive for meaning, orientation to the world, and salvation provides valuable theoretical material for understanding worldviews, so too with Durkheim's work on the way people view the world. Presented in the 'Introduction' to *The Elementary Forms of the Religious Life,* he argued that the very 'categories of understanding' – including 'time, space, number, personality' – by and through which people think, are generated by society itself: 'they correspond to the most universal properties of things ... they are like the framework of intelligence' ([1915] 1971:9). The organisation of these categories in each society is what Geertz's depicts as 'conceptions of a general order of existence', though he explicitly adds the 'aura of factuality' to the moods and motivations framing the conceptions. This 'aura of factuality' is sometimes problematic for religious devotees who speak of 'knowing' that their experience is true and incontrovertible. Its authenticity, their sense of God or some other divine source, is so palpable that they are unhappy, or even offended, by the word 'aura', which they interpret as somehow being false, inauthentic, or only appearing to be the case. Though Geertz's definition speaks more of the force than falsehood of experience some devotees instinctively decry it. At least this is an issue worth bearing in mind when considering his definition of religion in terms of people's identity and worldview.

Cantwell Smith

A different but highly informative approach to definition and religion comes from the Canadian scholar Wilfred Cantwell Smith who proposed replacing the term 'religion' with 'cumulative tradition' on the one hand and 'faith' on the other. In *The Meaning and End of Religion* (1963), the 'cumulative tradition' embraces such things as the history and development of doctrine, the material culture of architecture and objects, as well as ritual-symbolic behaviour, whereas 'faith' concerns the personal dynamics and emotional means by which people appropriate aspects of their cumulative tradition. He thought that people from one group tend to speak from their personal 'faith' to the 'cumulative tradition' of people from another group: and vice versa. For example, a Muslim might speak from the emotional commitment of the heart to the formal doctrinal formulae of a Catholic Christian: and vice versa. This places them on different wavelengths, but if each speaks in terms of their heart-feeling then quite a different communication ensues. This might, for example, enhance interfaith activity. Something similar can be argued if they share the cumulative experiences of their respective groups. This approach is intimately concerned with identity, and the way in which personal awareness and institutional factors interact, an issue of profound importance for Worldview Religious Studies.

Identity and Hans Mol (1922–2017)

One valuable approach to identity and religious devotees lies in the sociological work of Hans Mol who knew all too well how, 'the matter of definition plagues all scholars', especially in terms of the supernatural or natural nature of 'religion', leading him to account for 'religion' as 'the sacralisation of identity' (1976:1–4). This proposes that whatever phenomenon confers a sense of identity upon a group or person will be viewed with deep respect and a 'don't touch' attitude. Many phenomena that help build identity as a sure refuge amidst a world of potential confusion can be sacralised, including supernatural agents, places, objects, and experiences associated with them. These will be defended if attacked. Mol also emphasised caution over definitions of religion, something he says he avoided and 'refused to take seriously' for some time before, finally, aligning 'religion' with 'whatever sacralises identity' (1976:1,263, respectively). This reference to 'whatever' is important for Worldview Religious Studies for it can include secular or other validating bases on which life-perspectives may be based, flourish, and defended if attacked. It could easily be applied to the rise of the People's Republic of China in the twentieth and twenty-first centuries. Recent 'midlevel theory' drawn from attachment and terror management theories brings empirical evidence to substantiate Mol's 'don't touch' motif as in the proposition that 'it is first and foremost attachment-insecure individuals who erect rigid worldview defenses' (Granqvist, 2020:345, 224 respectively).

Phenomena that sacralise identity often take time to emerge as a new religious movement grows. For example, the early sects of Judaism that led to the separate Christian movement came to treat the human teacher, Jesus, as the divine second person of the Holy Trinity. Similarly, new believers with profound experiences of life and community transformation generated doctrinal statements regarding the power and status of the Holy Spirit. In Mol's sociological sense, Jesus's path from Nazareth to the right hand of God parallels a believer's path of new identity from sinner to salvation. As the new believer's sense of identity grows, and is sacralised, because of a sensed relationship with Jesus, so the believer accords high honour and status to the Lord. Both Saviour and the saved enter the field of sacralisation that is the church. New identities emerge in a mutual relationship of transformed relationships in which worship becomes appropriate behaviour and baptism into a new status with its own new Christian name established.

Processes of sacralisation that place certain identity-conferring phenomena beyond contradiction are, essentially, processes of meaning-making embedded within persons who are sustained and developed by groups and associations. This is not only where ritual-symbolism plays its part but where it, too, becomes subject to sacralisation, as in the bread and wine meal that becomes the Eucharist, Mass, or Holy Communion – as it is variously named in different traditions. The process of sacralisation, of investing much respect, dignity, and even devotion in the source of one's new identity has taken many directions. For example, the medieval philosophical-theological theory of transubstantiation depicts the very stuff of 'bread' becoming the very stuff of 'the Body of Christ', and wine becomes his blood. This one focal teaching, sustained by others concerning priesthood and church authority, has helped generate what is the Catholic Christian worldview, with Vatican City as its authenticating geographical centre. Something similar emerged with the Bible in association with the sixteenth-century Reformation split between Catholic and Protestant Christianity. Protestants vested considerable intellectual and emotional energy in arguing for the Bible as its own integral source of divine revelation, especially in terms of texts concerning faith and the justification of the sinner redeemed by the sacrificial death of Jesus, and of the Holy Spirit as enabling interpretation and appropriation of this message. In practice, the Bible becomes sacralised as its message helps transform the identity of the reader. This is one reason why the 'infallibility' of the Bible resembles the 'infallibility' of the Pope. Each stands as a symbolic embodiment of the salvation of believers and they will go to enormous lengths to defend that which makes them who they are.

Something similar has occurred in numerous sectarian movements, showing that the sacralisation of identity is a two-directional, mutual process. As a believer's self-identity increases through a perceived relationship with the identity-giver, so the believer views that source of identity with ever-increasing untouchable status. As a later chapter shows, it is now more common to speak of charisma as a quality of relationship between leader and devotee than simply of the intrinsic property of a leader. So too with sacralisation. This field of sacralisation could be explored in Islam where Mohammad, as the prophetic agent, and the Koran as the means of announcing and containing divine revelation foster Muslim identity. So too with the Sikh Gurus, the sacred text of the *Guru Granth*, and sacred community of the *Guru Panth*. Similarly with the prophet Joseph Smith, the Book of Mormon, and the rites of temples in the Church of Jesus Christ of Latter-day Saints. The power of sacralisation and identity helps interpret why some Christians and Muslims, for example, respond forcefully when certain images are vilified, for these symbols are not only seen as vehicles of divine revelation but as sources of a meaningful life for devotees. Because secular symbols, leaders, or texts may also sacralise the identity of individuals and groups, Mol's sacralisation hypothesis is of particular significance for worldview studies, not least when he reminds scholars of their own commitments, for he notes how a 'social scientific approach to religion' can itself become 'a worldview in which the researcher has invested a great deal of his emotions' (1976:250). In summary, Mol's *Identity and the Sacred: A Sketch for a New Social-Scientific Theory of Religion* offers one scheme that can be fruitfully explored as a basis for Worldview Studies.

Cognitive science

While Mol was initially wary of definitions, and Weber preferred describing behavioural types, Pascal Boyer, a cognitive anthropologist of a generation later, explicitly avoided strict definition of religion by arguing that there are templates in the brain for organising perceptions, and when some of these cluster together, they generate behaviour often defined as religion (2001). Instead of a single 'theory' or unique phenomenon of religion, numerous mental systems combine to produce highly adaptive worldviews. Drawing from evolutionary biology and cognitive science, he describes the underlying and unconscious processes as inference systems, including moral-emotional, verbal communication, intuitive psychology, social exchange, and Person-File systems. Crucial to Boyer's case is that no inference system exists for analysing abstract issues as such. So while inference systems may engage with the environment and give a sense of the presence of ancestors, gods, or spirits, there is no in-built means of validating that impression. Practically speaking, 'the intuitive psychology system treats ancestors (or Gods) as intentional agents, exchange system treats them as exchange partners, moral system treats them as potential witnesses to moral action, Person-File system treats them as distinct individuals' (Boyer, 2001). In terms of the practical impact of these systems, he sees prayer being grounded in mental capacities for verbal exchange, with promises made to intuited supernatural agents pivoting around inferences on reciprocity and embedded dynamics concerning morals and emotions fostering ethical behaviour. This approach is quite different from either philosophy or theology and is more dependent on recent developments in brain science with its practical experiments on how people respond to their environment. Other scholars adopt variations of this kind of cognitive approach and accept the natural rather than divine basis of 'religion' (Atran, 2002, McCauley and Thomas, 2002, Tremlin, 2006), but not all cognitive-based thinkers conclude their studies solely on the naturalness of religion, as the following two cases of Seybold and Asma demonstrate.

Divine reality and practical agnosticism

Seybold (2007) accepts the neuroscientific–psychological accounts of mental processing but retains God in his total life narrative. He tells of his personal experience of Christian conversion when he 'sensed God's presence in a way that I did not feel a few minutes earlier'. This was something 'real to me' (2007:75). In none of this research, does he find 'a serious challenge to religious faith', indeed, 'the truth revealed in nature will not and cannot conflict with the truth revealed in scripture' (2007:137,142). His account of scientific research on parts of the brain associated with such experiences, which he describes as 'innate spirituality', are often allied with the practice of prayer and meditation. He argues that 'if God exists and has created humans for the purpose of enjoying a relationship with him … there should be some physical mechanism to allow for the development of that relationship' (2007:85). He aligns himself with the position that 'brain structures and networks implicated in religious experience might have evolved because there is a spiritual world' (2007:81). This is a clear example of how a foundational hypothesis, in this case, a Christian faith claim, becomes the driver of other information. In just the same way, of course, someone else might assume that there is no divine overriding causal basis for interpreting things. What we need to be careful about in such cases is the way in which knowledge is stacked and interpreted, what takes priority, and how priority directs thinking.

Somewhere between Seybold and Boyer lies Asma. This philosopher owns extensive knowledge of cognitive science, and once used it in his opposition to traditional forms of religion, but now contextualises it in the light of personal circumstances. Here, it is not a conversion at an evangelistic rally, but a father in an accident and emergency hospital with his son's life in peril that elicits Asma's existential testimony. This brings him to disagree with 'the radical atheists' because 'the irrationality of religion does not render it unacceptable or valueless', for he now identifies 'religion' as having 'emotionally therapeutic power': being rather 'like art' its behaviours have 'direct access to our emotional lives in ways that science does not'. While agreeing with Richard Dawkins and Sam Harris that religion 'fails miserably at the bar of rational validity', he reckons this to be the 'wrong bar', arguing that 'most religious beliefs are not true. But here's the crux. The emotional brain doesn't care' (Asma, 2018:2–5). When in distress, 'neuroscience … didn't alleviate my anguish and desperation in the emergency room with my son' (2018:211); unlike many engaged in theological and philosophical arguments who seek to defend or attack 'religion', he takes a different position, expressing his own sense of 'needing a crutch', whether in prayer or meditation to get through life's hardships (2018:57).

Attachment theory and religion

Asma's case provides a natural lead into discussing attachment theories and religion, the attachment of parent and child, and of an anxious parent to a sense of a supportive environment. Attachment theory arose within psychological approaches to animal and especially to human development where helpless babies require extensive care to thrive; nurturing and protective parent-figures in mother, father, and wider family and community, are vital for survival. Sigmund Freud and especially John Bowlby and others developed 'attachment' theories, discussing the nature of different kinds of attachment of person to person, and what that means when one of them dies (Davies, 2017:53–78). That work on bereavement has tended to remain separate from other attachment-driven theories analysing a variety of relationships with God as an attachment figure (Granqvist, 2021), an issue pursued in a later chapter on ancestors.

Conclusion

This chapter has collected some key definitional approaches to both religion and worldviews, highlighting their capacity to bring meaning to life and sustain people in distress. It has drawn from a variety of academic perspectives and developed concepts and theories that will now be complemented by further conceptual tools in the following chapter, where destiny, supported by hope, come to the fore in supporting the idea of Worldview Religious Studies.

3 Destiny, ritual-symbol, and gift

Introduction

This chapter's topics aim to increase the battery of theoretical concepts vital for a Worldviews Religious Studies. Beginning with a distinctive formula dealing with ideas, emotions, values, identity, belief, and the notion of destiny, it addresses 'hope', ritual-symbolism, and especially reciprocity or gift theory as the most illuminating means of studying human interaction and ideas of salvation. Developing earlier accounts of ethos and mood, emotions are also stressed to offset much Western thinking that has frequently accentuated rational approaches to religious life and worldviews (Davies, 2011).

Destiny, identity, and hope

This chapter also stresses the idea of destiny as a characteristic feature of many worldviews. Both destiny and identity share in the meaning-making processes underlying human development and evolving cultural understandings of life. This needs some explanation, beginning with the fact that people are ever surrounded by words, often simple names for things, some of which grow in complexity as they are invested with emotional significance. Here I propose that such emotion-pervaded ideas be identified as 'values'. Though the notion of 'value' has an extensive history in several disciplines as Wyschogrod has shown (1998), here the emotion-addition stands as a key feature. To it is added the proposition that if and when such a 'value' contributes to a sense of identity, an identity factor or 'belief' emerges. This need not be a 'religious' belief, but could be political, gender-linked, or in today's cultural pre-occupation 'environmental'. These identity-conferring 'beliefs' at the personal level usually also complement community worldviews. Still, there remains one further meaning-making level to consider as part of Worldview Religious Studies, that of

DOI: 10.4324/9781003242437-5

destiny: this level can be equated with 'religious belief', or simply be designated as a destiny factor. Most world religions carry this category, often because they engage with death and some notion of an afterlife. However, it is because some scholars disavow 'religious' categories, but still wish to speak of some 'ultimate' meaningfulness that reference to 'destiny factor' can be preferred over 'religious' belief. All this can be expressed in this following schema.

Idea–destiny formula
Idea
Idea + emotion = value
Value informing identity = belief
Belief framing destiny = religious belief or destiny factor

As a thought experiment exemplifying this scheme, one might take any word, let us say 'tree', and ask whether it is just an 'idea', or is perhaps invested with some emotion to generate a 'value', or may even constitute more of a 'belief' by contributing to a sense of identity. Finally, there might be a context where the identity-linked tree also involves a destiny factor. Historically, the Christian tradition has elaborated on the trees in the biblical Garden of Eden and in heavenly Paradise as well as seeing the Cross as the tree of life that hosted the crucified Saviour (Evans, 2014). Elsewhere the Norse tree of sacrifice, Christmas Trees, or trees used in woodland-burial practice, all carry a symbolic and emotional load, just as today, trees at large are easily symbolised in ecological–environmental terms as the earth's lungs.

Narrative and worldviews

All such trees embed forceful stories, theologies, and scientific messages, often pointing to narratives informing worldviews, especially when encountered in sacred texts believed to be the very medium through which the divine is revealed to humankind. The copying, printing, and devotional use of such texts often parallel the importance of commentaries and interpretations for devotees' daily life. Sacred narratives range from doctrinal and mythological accounts of key scriptural motifs to local storytelling, performances at festivals, and liturgical events. Songs and hymns frequently carry narrative messages, enhancing them through the medium of music. Some scholars have pondered not only the 'deliberate artistry' but also the 'playfulness' evident as biblical authors explore variations on the theme they want to convey to believing communities (Alter, 1981:155). Whether in sacred mode or the wide community sharing of national anthems, 'Happy

Birthday', and folk-songs, music frequently intensifies their relatively simple yet emotionally charged messages.

Destiny and hope

Destiny is a concept that has played an occasional but restricted role in Religious Studies (Holm and Bowker, 1994, Davies and Drury, 1997). It is, however, of direct relevance for worldview studies, especially when approached in terms of human creativity constrained by perception 'of the dividedness or unsatisfactoriness of life', making it intrinsic to 'the nature of human nature', whether in terms of key worldviews concerned with illusion and the need for enlightenment, or sin demanding redemption, or, indeed, secularist traditions demanding revolution in social organisation (Davies, 1994:1–8). For these contexts, destiny is frequently framed by issues of ethics, commandments, or expectations of ancestral forces, complemented by notions of salvation rooted in cosmic processes of merit or in saviour figures. As such destiny is an anticipated future state of identity. Some have even spoken of 'chance transformed into destiny' as and when some apparently random event becomes deeply significant for a community (Krauss, 2003:201). Allied with hope as its emotional present tense and existential dynamic, destiny helps reduce the fear occasioned by life's fragmentations (Davies, 2011:191–202). In this, hope at the cultural level of life parallels the drive to survive at its biological level. When hope combines with an anticipated destiny, an emotionally satisfying context emerges for the meaning-making achieved within personal identity.

This kind of prospective destiny scenario may appear strange within the loosely secular society of Great Britain where the destiny element is eliminated or considerably reduced, leaving some with a strong identity-focus that correlates with self-description as 'spiritual but not religious'. This stresses the values sustaining their sense of identity but not set within traditional streams of religions that offer a destiny frame for identity. Here the ideas–destiny formula is useful for understanding secularisation as a process of reduction of the destiny factor and, along with it, lack of interest in afterlife dynamics. Indeed, some have argued that westernised secular mind-sets tend to marginalise or even neutralise the very nature of death, in preference to a focused engagement in life-issues (Bauman, 1992).

Although, in Mol's terms, this 'spiritual but not religious' identity is not sacralised through traditional religious institutions, it often reveals a defensive 'keep-off' response not unlike some sex-gender, ethnicity and colour, or ecology–environmental perspectives. However, recent demographic shifts, not least in the UK, find growing Islamic, Pentecostal–Charismatic, and more conservative Christians, possessing a strong destiny dimension allied with ideas of an immortal soul, judgement, and resurrection. Moreover, the recent burgeoning of environmentalism affords its own form of 'natural' destiny that will emerge later when discussing the innovation of woodland burial and ecological aspects of a natural worldview. Such mixed communities involve both grand narratives that outline destiny for entire communities and smaller groups and individuals with their own explanatory rationales in narrative and ritual-symbolic forms; some speak of these as 'master narratives' (Chater and Donnellan, 2020:117).

Narrative often drives the inviting notion of destiny, not least in major nation-states and their political–economic vicissitude. For example, Kay and King's influential study of risk in today's complex world gives considerable prominence to narrative theory, to good and bad narratives: 'storytelling is how humans normally try to interpret complex situations. And such storytelling is universal' (2020:216). King had been Governor of the Bank of England 2003–2013, and Kay an Oxford and London academic. Embracing chimpanzee communication, American presidents, and anthropological reciprocity theory, as well as comparing daytime 'economics' and night-time 'stories' among !Kung bushpeople, they contextualise leaders of international companies to show how 'emotions and human cognition are not separate processes' especially in the development of 'conviction narratives' (2020:227). No better study reveals the narrative force of ideas that feed into high-level drivers of worldviews that are not apparently 'religious'.

Ritual – symbolism

But what of 'religious' narratives? While some undergo extensive theological–philosophical refinement taking them beyond the comprehension of ordinary devotees, many exert considerable popular force when sung or chanted. Their musical form commands a significance all of its own, exemplified through many mantras, prayer-formulae, and creeds, all embedded within ritual-symbolic behaviour, leaving it impossible to consider dominant narratives without thinking of how key ideas and emotions carried by them contribute to Worldview Religious Studies. Whether thinking about the Christian Eucharist, Islamic Hajj, the Olympic Games and national anthems, birthday parties, and many other events, ritual behaviour and symbolic acts combine, making it wise to combine them and speak of ritual-symbolism. While there are many theories of ritual and symbolism, indeed 'Ritual Studies' has developed as something of its own specialism (Grimes, 1990), some foundational concepts need highlighting here, leaving others for later attention.

Rites of passage

The best-known theoretical account of ritual is captured in the phrase 'rites of passage' derived from a 1909 essay by Arnold van Gennep (1873–1957) in which he developed a three-part scheme for analysing changes in social status as people move from birth to death. They occupy many social statuses whether as child, adult, graduate, marriage partner, professional, or retired, until they finally die and achieve status as ancestor, as deceased, or as a memory. Van Gennep's threefold scheme depicts a starting point (pre-liminal), a transition period (liminal), and an ensuing post-liminal status. Where 'limen' is derived from the Latin for 'threshold'. A person is separated from one status and undergoes a period of segregated apartness in which training or other experiences are gained before being reincorporated into society with a new status. One scheme might show how a school pupil (pre-liminal) becomes an undergraduate (liminal) and finally a graduate (post-liminal). This may involve a matriculation ceremony granting a person undergraduate status, many liminal experiences of student life, before a graduation ceremony confers the status of graduate holding the university's degree. Similarly, a person may hold lay status in a religious community before being trained as a priest and then ordained, or a civilian admitted to the army, trained, and then becoming a soldier. In some traditional societies, a boy may be removed from ordinary life, experience some hardships and even pain and some distress, before being deemed ready to re-enter social life as a man; similar events can also frame the life of girl into woman, and married woman into mother. Van Gennep saw such events as involving changes that can involve anxiety if not actual danger, and spoke of 'society' taking people by the hand and leading them through these transitions. Depending upon the ultimate purpose of the triple-process, he thought that one or other of the three phases would predominate. A marriage rite, for example, might stress the separation of bride from her original family group as she moves into her husband's family, or a funeral might emphasise the incorporation of the deceased into the realm of the ancestors or into heaven. In all this, van Gennep stressed status and status change, placing relatively little emphasis on emotional feelings or the psychology of status shifts.

Liminality and communitas

It was not until some time after van Gennep's death that his notion gained a wider public as in William Golding's novel *Rites of Passage* (1980), though the concept's growing familiarity sometimes led to inappropriate application. Much as 'charisma' in sociology, and 'mindfulness' in psychology, both rites of passage and liminality in anthropology, have been subject to a kind of conceptual creep. The British anthropologist Victor Turner (1920–1983) developed the notion of liminality as a social context by portraying initiates as experiencing a sense of shared emotion and mutual unity. This he termed *communitas* and thereby brought a sense of emotion and human feeling to the more status–only focus of van Gennep's liminal context. *Communitas* become the feeling-state of liminality. Turner had long been interested in literature, theatre, and dramatic performance, and this combined with his non-combatant bomb-disposal military service and sense of comradeship amidst danger helped foster his sense of the dynamic arena of ritual and symbols.

Symbolic polarity

Turner spoke of symbols as having two poles, the ideological pole encapsulating 'ideas' or 'doctrines', and the sensory pole embracing human senses and emotions. Such symbols are also multi-vocal or polysemic (Latin and Greek derived), carrying many meanings. In a term derived from Freud, he also spoke of 'condensation' to note the clustering of meaning and emotions around symbols that help forge what can be seen as a group's worldview. This terminology could now help to develop interesting accounts of the Jewish Passover Meal, Islamic Hajj, or Christian Holy Communion. This last case would have bread as a symbol with two 'poles': an ideological pole capturing much theology of Christ's incarnation, sacrificial status as 'lamb of God who takes away the sins of the world' as also of 'gift', offering, and sacrifice; while the sensory pole captures the visual, auditory, postural, and gustatory (tasting and eating) dimensions of rites that mark what is sometimes called 'lived experience'. Here Christians 'eat their ideas' as sensory and ideological dynamics unite in ritual-symbolic moments contributing not only to people's sense of identity but also their destiny – as the priest says something like 'The Body of Christ keep you in eternal life'.

Embodiment

Whether as Christians at their Eucharist, Muslims on their *Hajj,* Mormons at their temples, or Sikhs being initiated, the body becomes the arena of ideological and sensory interaction or, in Cantwell Smith's terms, the integrative focus of their cumulative tradition and personal dynamics of faith. Embodiment theory is integrative and avoids separating mind and body, or soul and body. It embraces ideas of *habitus* and *gestus* that capture typical ways of 'being' and 'expressing' group participation (Davies, 2002:19–52). This includes carriage, speech, and general behaviour of persons as they relate to their group's core cultural values as anthropologist Mary Douglas did much to describe and interpret (1966 and 1970), with consequences for ongoing development of her ideas (Duschinsky et al., 2016).

Reciprocity–gift theory

Ritual-symbols also pervade and constitute much of life. Acts of mutual give-and-take generate and sustain identity and social cohesion in everyday life, captured in expressions such as – 'what goes around, comes around', invoking some natural equivalence ensuring that sooner or later people get what they deserve. When disasters strike those deemed to be 'good' then the question of fairness arises because attitudes of getting 'what they deserve' are grounded in the rationale of everyday life where 'give and take' parallels a sense of fair-play, popular justice, and a simple sense of social obligation. This was theoretically explained in reciprocity or 'gift' theory by anthropologist Marcel Mauss (1872–1950). His seminal study *The Gift, Forms and Functions of Exchange in Archaic Society* ([1925] 1966) laid a foundation for gift theory by identifying a threefold obligation to give, receive, and return a gift in a process that helps create society itself. Mauss was part of a group surrounding Emile Durkheim that saw society as a 'whole' or 'total social process', as in his and Henri Hubert's *Sacrifice Its Nature and Function* ([1899] 1964) and its 'gift-theory of sacrifice'.

Gifts can be physical objects, food, periods of time, knowledge and insight, care for others or life itself. Ordinary life exists in and through processes of reciprocity, the symbols used in them, and the identity grounded in such associations, exchanges, and alliances. Such symbols participate in what they represent, and are not simply signs indicative of something else. Blood, for example, is often used as a symbol, gaining its potency from its actual reality in physical experience. So too, with water, or notions of mother, father, brother, and the like. To define a symbol as participating in that which it represents is to echo the formula aligning emotion to an idea to generate a value. So symbols are not 'arbitrary signs' such as the green traffic light that could equally have another colour or even the word 'go'. Symbols often carry an accumulated load of cultural emotion absent in a sign. In religious contexts, they frequently intensify ordinary aspects of life. Bread in the Catholic Mass, for example, becomes the body of Christ through a prayer of consecration.

The threefold obligation – alienable gifts – force

Gifts associated with Mauss' threefold obligation are alienable, can be costed, bought and sold, and involve cycles of obligation continuing into the future. We use gifts to initiate or to mark special relationships in birthdays, engagements, marriage, etc., and there is always some degree of appropriateness in the gifts. Although we often say 'it is the thought that counts' we do not really believe that. Mauss spoke of a 'force' present in a gift that demands a return gift in the future. Both 'force' and 'obligation' are important for expressing the emotional nature of human relationships, including Durkheim's idea of society as a moral community. For Durkheim, 'society' and 'moral community' are practically synonymous and mark the emotional attachments experienced in communities.

The fourth obligation – inalienable 'gifts'

Inalienable gifts, by contrast, lie beyond market value or price. The consecrated Eucharistic 'bread' cannot be bought at a market, it is 'priceless' with deep meaning for devotees. So too with objects of 'sentimental value' passed down and between generations. In religious traditions, they are precious to guardians of core ritual-symbols. Priesthood, for example, might be regarded as an inalienable gift that has to be received and passed on but cannot be bought or sold.

The UK's National Health Service at the core of Britain's Welfare State is similar, making the public and some politicians deeply concerned if there is any talk of 'selling out' to private business concerns. In terms of education, the relationship between teacher and student, and certainly between devotee and guru in the Indian traditions, holds teaching, knowledge, and even wisdom, as a precious 'gift' to be passed on. At the more personal level, inalienable gifts, rings, and other objects constitute family heirlooms that materialise our memories of others.

This distinction between alienable and inalienable entities is important especially as developed by anthropologist Maurice Godelier (1999). He described how inalienable gifts, often in the form of ritual-symbols, link believers with the prime values of their community in terms of their origins, ancestors, deities, or social heroes, often through narratives that give meaning and energy to their life. Issues of status are often aligned with alienable and inalienable contexts because the social worth of people is proved through their behaviour. Sometimes, societies accord special praise for going beyond the call of duty and grant special honours or privileges that are probably best interpreted as examples of inalienable cultural gifts as chapter four shows for ideas of salvation. One valuable way of considering the core values of cultural traditions and their worldviews is Rappaport's notion of 'Ultimate Sacred Postulates' enshrined in such utterances as the Jewish *Shema* – 'Hear O Israel the Lord our God the Lord is One', or the Muslim *Shahada*, the first pillar of Islam, in which the devotee confesses that 'there is no god but God, and … Mohammed is the messenger of God'

(1999:277). Much the same could be said of early Christianity's working 'creed' – 'Jesus is Lord', or of Buddhists taking a threefold refuge in the Buddha, Dharma, and Sangha. Relating in different ways to what has already been said of Otto, Mol, and Asma, Rappaport's analysis is invaluable in analysing such ritual-symbolic realms of devotees revealed in the 'remarkable spectacle' of

> *The unfalsifiable supported by the undeniable yields the unquestionable, which transforms the dubious, the arbitrary, and the conventional Into the correct, the necessary, and the natural.*
>
> (Rappaport 1999:405. Original emphasis)

This is not a negative criticism of religious worldviews any more than it would be of political outlooks or ideas of 'democracy' that are conventional and accepted by experience and tradition.

Paradigmatic scenes and worldviews

In Rappaport, we find one potential characteristic of a worldview, the presence of functional Ultimate Sacred Postulates that appear in pledges of allegiance to country or major institutions. At the personal level, they also appear in vows of fidelity to marriage partners, often made through verbal utterances framed by ritual-symbol events. Ultimate Sacred Postulates are frequently expressed within paradigmatic scenes, or cameo performances enshrining cultural commitments whether in Christmas Nativity scenes performed in thousands of schools and churches, or by Shi'a groups of Muslim's in many parts of the world practising self-beating in memory of their Imam Hussain's martyrdom at *Karbala* (AD 680, Christian dating; 61 AH Islamic dating).

Indifference and uncertainty

Despite obligations driving reciprocal relations, and people's commitment to Ultimate Sacred Postulates, some remain indifferent or unsure as to their life orientations. Though indifference is a neglected topic in an age when many pride themselves on their opinions and active engagement, it remains significant for the study of worldviews because it acknowledges an anticipated diversity amongst people. People sometimes change attitudes as they age, often with a degree of uncertainty replacing earlier absolutes. Just how indifference and uncertainty play out in a person's life is a complex issue, but it is worth bearing in mind especially when sociological analyses either force binary options, as between belief and non-belief, or provide no opportunity to acknowledge indifference (Davies, 2015:378–81).

Conclusion

This chapter linked ideas, emotions, values, and identity in a discussion of destiny. Combined with some basic elements of ritual-symbolism and reciprocity theory, it has provided a basis for the next chapter's consideration of merit as a prime concept when discussing evil and salvation. Together, these chapters will complete the preliminary work needed before Part Two presents its approach to Religious Worldview Studies.

4 Evil, merit, and salvation

Introduction

Ideas of evil and salvation underlie all worldviews, where evil depicts perceived flaws in existence, and salvation methods for overcoming them. These concepts are not restricted to familiar doctrines of religious traditions but also apply to secular ideologies that posit problems of existence and society and ways of resolving them. Moreover, ideas of merit often play a part in the dynamic relationship between 'evil' and 'salvation'. Though some might object to using these terms because of their long association with religion, there is considerable advantage in widening their use within worldview religious studies to reveal similarity of meaning-making processes in any society (Davies, 1984).

Merit–Demerit

Both merit and demerit surround social life and become intensified when the model of earthly justice is reflected in divine or supernatural justice applied to a transcendent realm. Whether in a day of divine judgement, notably in the Jewish–Christian–Islamic worlds, or in impersonal processes of *karma*, evident in Indian-derived traditions affecting the state of a transmigrating self, a person's destiny hangs on the merit accounted to them. The crucial point is that ordinary schemes grounded in daily values and identity are intensified in the context of destiny as merit becomes associated with the status of salvation. What might be called ordinary merit-capital, gained from proper social obligations, is intensified in religious or soteriological-capital. Just as a good citizen acquires a good reputation resulting in cultural-merit so a religious devotee, following the commandments or path laid down in their religion may obtain salvation – merit. As the karmic worldview of chapter nine will show, not only can merit may be made in and through ritual behaviour, but that very activity can also provide its own

DOI: 10.4324/9781003242437-6

positive emotional outcome. Making merit, as in giving gifts to monks in Buddhism, should not be separated from the benefit felt by simply performing a ritual act. Likewise, negative acts generate negative merit.

The balancing of positive and negative merit to obtain destiny's goal occupies many religious traditions, and this is problematic since they often depict people as failing in their obedience to divine laws, principles, and commands. Christianity and Islam, for example, speak of sins as a kind of accumulation of evil that will deplete a person's destiny status either entirely or for a purgative period. Christianity's hell or heaven, or Islam's 'fire' or paradise garden depict awful scenes of punishment, pain, and suffering, directed by angelic credit–debit accounts. Muslims seek a balance to the advantage of the devotee. Indian traditions reckon good and bad karma to affect the cycle of transmigration. Catholic Christianity has also engaged in this kind of moral-logic with ideas of purgatory and of hell, as well as of the treasury of merits of the church accumulated by the self-sacrificial actions of saints and martyrs, and which can – through indulgences – even be accessed by sinful believers. This was a significant issue in the Protestant Reformation that accorded all merit to Christ alone and saw salvation as the free granting of his merit to believers through their faith. In Buddhism, lifetime and dedicated short-term periods as monks allow for the making of merit that can be shared with lay people.

Compassion, Grace, and Humility Response

However, the market-like making and sharing of merit, reminiscent of alienable gift exchange, is not the only sphere of soteriological-capital, for many traditions possess more inalienable-like processes of salvation in which devotees' demerits are transcended by divine fiat. In ancient Israel, *Yahweh* delivers the chosen people into their promised land despite their moral culpability. Christianity describes Jesus delivering believers from sin through his sacrificial living and death. The figure of Amida Buddha in Chinese and Japanese Pure Land Schools affords deliverance from karma-like evil through insightful moments of trust. Somewhat analogously, the Tibetan Buddhist tradition hosts the ongoing reincarnation known as the Dalai Lama as an aid of compassion for needy humanity. Sikh traditions speak of the grace of the True Guru bringing bliss to the one caught in the divine glance. Other mystical traditions, including Sufis in Islam, bring a sense of union with the divine to predominate over rule-based living. In these contexts, the very nature of compassion and grace share a family resemblance in the benevolence of supernatural agents.

Comparatively speaking, not only do ordinary societies flourish when their members obey rules and accrue merit-enhancing status but so do religious traditions with their destiny-reaching goals. If and when certain individuals exceed reasonable expectation, they may be singled out for special honours and, surprisingly perhaps, often respond with expressions of humility, something identifiable as the 'humility response' (Davies, 2011:158–9). In ordinary life, the granting of an award involves singling out someone for praise and recognition as in the Monarch's system of honours of the British Empire. It involves receiving a medal from the Monarch along with the citation in the media and publicity in the community from which they come. There is a sense in which this cultural case of Royal recognition indicates its own form of an 'establishment' worldview.

In what might loosely be called the academic 'worldview', degrees reflect something similar. Students work for a degree that becomes theirs by right, merited through work done and exams passed in an alienable market-place of knowledge, fees, and obligation. A select few, however, are invested with an honorary degree, and while this is in recognition of their outstanding contribution to society or scholarship, it still comes at the will of the university. No one can apply for it, it comes to them, perhaps even as a surprise. This academic worldview prompts analogy with religious worldviews because both the honorary degree and grace accorded by a deity to a devotee express the inalienable self-generated goodwill of the university or deity and not the threefold obligation of giving, receiving, return-gift, of alienable processes.

Evil and worldviews

But what of problematic contexts and the anxiety occasioned by negative merit and its destiny potential, since people experience distress in a world that is not as humans would like it to be? Indeed, a characteristic of mythology and religious ideologies lies in the flawed aspect of existence. Natural calamity, accidents, disasters, sickness, and death frustrate the very nature of life. The untimely death of infants and mothers in childbirth, of parents and partners in their prime, all prompt questions of why bad things happen. Their apparent randomness is often hard to accept and fosters ideas of malevolence whether through the evil-eye, witchcraft, evil-spirits, or the sheer malice of others. Betrayal, too, can be a profound evil in a person or community's existence, as can an individual's thought that their own bad behaviour has caused their misfortune. And above all these things war and the devastation nation inflicts on nation has caused immeasurable suffering and death, often involving the clash of worldviews.

If a worldview is to flourish, it needs to provide not only some explanatory schemes for perceived flaws and inadequacies, but also some coping procedures, often in ritual-symbolic forms. Though too simple a generalisation, 'western' schemes set the flaw in a historical–theological narrative of creation, fall, redemption, and future world transformation, just as some 'eastern' schemes identify flaws in perception and illusion demanding mental transformation in enlightenment. It is against such existential negativities that ideas of salvation arise, fostering the capacity to overcome, transcend, contextualise, and cope with evils at large, often doing so through supernatural saviour figures and associated ritual-symbolic processes. Today, the potential 'evils' of global warming, pandemics, and wars assume a high profile and invite new approaches to human meaning-making, identity, and destiny. Here, a broadly conceived use of 'salvation' may be of considerable value in embracing secular as well as religious worldviews within this book's remit of Worldview Religious Studies.

Salvation

The idea of salvation needs some explanation in terms of Worldview Religious Studies because its strong association with 'world religions' might be seen by some to disqualify it for 'worldview' use. Fortunately, this is not only a misguided idea but strengthens the reason for adopting it once it is approached in terms of plausibility theory as a social scientific perspective grounded in the sociology of knowledge (Berger, 1969). Plausibility theory accounts for human meaning-making, integrating rational and emotional dynamics of life, and stands as a higher order or umbrella concept for both 'religious' and 'secular' enterprises in explaining the world and the place of humans in it. This perspective prompts the question of how the human drive for meaning has so often taken cultural forms described as salvation as analysed in *Meaning and Salvation in Religious Studies* (Davies, 1984), continued in *Anthropology and Theology* (Davies, 2002), and now appearing here in alliance with the notion of destiny to capture the emotional and intellectual satisfaction of desire and transcendence of 'evils'. Echoing Rappaport's discussion that combines deutero-truths with Ultimate Sacred Postulates, as well as Boyer's view of cognitive processes as not possessing the sheer capacity to answer the higher-order questions of the existence of supernatural entities, this approach to salvation reveals human beings dealing with deeply negative aspects of life through philosophy, theology, and ritual-symbolic processes. Here Christian, Islamic, Hindu, Humanist, and Communist cultural contexts all provide means for coping with pain, tragedy, loss, death, and an overall meaning of things. For some, the drive for meaning lifts the human desire to 'know' beyond ordinary life circumstances to the realms of destiny whether in heaven or a perfected society. While this is usually an elite venture, many do not achieve 'salvation' by rational–propositional–textual means but through devotional, ritual, and ethical practices. Even the intrinsic satisfaction of learning and knowing is often gained within the ritual contexts of academic worldviews.

Historically, this paralleling of thought and ritual action has been enormously successful within religious worldviews where devotees encounter doctrinal teaching within ritual-symbolic behaviour and are exhorted to practise or 'perform' their truths in ethical action. Together, these allow the force, energy, and commitment of life to be intensified, appropriated, and personally embodied, often sustained through personified saviour figures or processes that incorporate ideas of merit in opposing evil. Meanwhile, music, movement, and the manipulation of bodies integrate the ideological and sensory dynamics of ritual-symbolic events, with the concept of 'flow' being one theoretical account of how practised performance yields its own satisfaction (Csikszentmihaly, ([1974] 1991).

Conclusion

This chapter has explored ideas of evil and salvation through a sociological perspective on meaning-making, allied with ideas of merit, ritual, and ethics. Its emphasis on 'salvation', sociologically defined, adds to the numerous theoretical tools provided in previous chapters to enable this book to move into its second part which categorises worldviews within a broad framework of Religious Studies.

Part 2
Worldview Types

5 Types of worldview

Introduction

Part One discussed forms of meaning-making, identity, and destiny; the 'evil' of negative constraints that frustrate them; and 'salvation' as a means of overcoming such negativities. Part Two now approaches Worldview Religious Studies through a classification of worldviews that seeks to encompass the enormity of groups, movements, and processes, whether primarily religious, secular, or mixed, that flood the history of the world. This provisional classification has been composed with Religious Studies and some theology and ethics topics in mind and, in technical language, takes the form of a classification or collection of 'ideal types'. The idea of an ideal type was favoured by sociologist Max Weber as a way of pinpointing key features of some phenomenon, and is useful for providing thumbnail sketches or cameos that capture prime elements of similar movements. This exploratory typology will doubtless need improvement but, for the moment, it can prompt thinking and discussions.

Because human life is complex and subject to change we may find some worldviews clear and explicit on positive and negative dynamics of life while others seem vaguer. Traditional societies that have evolved over millennia are likely to possess relatively implicit views of the world and codes of life that are taken for granted, and dispersed across many aspects of behaviour that celebrate 'meaning' and confront negativity. By contrast, new religious movements that have recently emerged in protest against some pre-existing worldview are likely to have some very explicit formulations and codes of life on the contested meanings, but these take much longer to explain wider aspects of life. For example, in Mormonism, Marxist–Leninist communism, feminism, or environmentalism, it is easier to identify key texts, manifestoes, activities, and ideas of what they deem 'evil', than their attitudes to, say, stamp-collecting. In modern, complex, multicultural societies, we can expect to find a mix of perspectives with points of agreement and difference

DOI: 10.4324/9781003242437-8

between them. Indeed, we might even ask if 'multiculturalism' is, itself, a worldview. Still, as abstract categories, each worldview type may relate to several identifiable movements that share a basic affinity. Depending on that shared element, what follows may sometimes differ from the classifications offered by previous studies, as when Animism, Shamanism, Shinto, and Environmentalism are here arranged together under the natural worldview category with which we begin the typology.

Cultural classification – worldview classification

The typological approach is, itself, a formal example of the cultural classification of phenomena that is foundational to all human activities. While the issue of whether any of these types should be described as religious or not is highly problematic, chapter three's progressive 'idea to destiny' scheme affords one helpful signpost, especially when aligned with issues of 'evil' or severe constraints upon meaning-making. Everything depends upon the rationale underlying any classification. For example, when the great Swedish Professor Linnaeus (1707–1778) created his Latin classification of plants, naming and scientifically organising types in his garden in Uppsala, his essentially scientific venture was unlike the intrinsic classification of plants and animals in the biblical mythology of Genesis. Though son of a clergyman and one of the most remarkable scholars of the entire eighteenth century, his was not a theological exercise in identity and destiny but an attempt to bring order to the multiplicity of plants in the world. Still, whether in Linnaeus' botanical garden or the biblical Garden of Eden, the issue of classification always emerges in a desire to organise life. The extent to which a classificatory system that simply 'organises' things may be adopted and framed by issues of emotion, identity, and destiny, is the extent to which it plays a religious role. To establish an ordering of plants is not the same as believing that order to be divinely ordained.

Typology / Classification

Against that background, and Ninian Smart's broad comparative religion of the worldview concept, and Droogers and Harskamp's more recent anthropology-influenced book in chapter one, the following scheme sets out its own eight-fold typology. This identifies key features of orientations to the world that provide meaning, hope, identity, and even a sense of destiny while not forgetting negative aspects of existence and corresponding methods of coping with them. The first two hold distinctive relevance to early twenty-first-century concerns with ecology and environmentalism. In contexts of mixed populations, some will be found alongside or as dominant over others, but together they all embrace phenomena found across the world. While this sketched outline gives a sense of the combination of topics that appear more fully in later chapters, some of these are given more attention than others depending on the number of phenomena included in each type.

1. Natural
2. Scientific
3. Ancestral
4. Karmic
5. Prophetic-sectarian
6. Mystical
7. Ideological
8. Ludic

Natural worldviews

To speak of 'nature' is, from the outset, to be reminded that each culture classifies the world in different ways so that, for example, when western Europeans speak in a binary way of 'culture and nature', they already divide entities in ways that many societies would find alien. Here the domains of Animism, Shamanism, Shinto, and Environmentalism are brought together because of their affinity with 'natural' aspects of the world.

Animism

Animism rests on the idea that the world is full of forces, sometimes described as spirits that may be viewed as relatively impersonal or more personal energies. The influential nineteenth-century scholar Sir Edward Burnett Tylor coined the term 'Animism' to cover this attitude towards, or awareness of, the dynamic forcefulness of the environment. Trees, rivers, mountains, any other phenomena are treated as special, with respect, and perhaps even with awe. Key to this perspective is that humans are interactively part of this environment.

Shamanism

Relationships with some of the invisible 'natural' world are evident in the phenomenon of *Shamanism*, where certain individuals are believed to have the capacity to engage with spirit forces, often through trance states. Shamanism is widespread in the world today, both in its ancient heartland of Siberia, as also in South Korea, and numerous South American contexts.

For idiosyncratic historical reasons, it has not been customary in the UK to speak of 'Shamanism' in Africa, but there are practices there that could easily be subsumed in this title. Key to traditional Shamanism is the goal of some kind of therapy or desire to assist the community. The shaman is often a form of healer. There is, too, a domain often described as Neo-Shamanism practised by western groups today in a kind of mirroring of 'traditional' Shamanism, and frequently employing musical rhythm in drumming and chanting to enter a trance state as a form of transcendence, of experiencing something beyond that of the everyday life-world.

Shinto

Shinto embraces a worldview that frames much ritual activity in Japan key to which is the sense that 'nature' as a domain is not some kind of passive realm but owns its own *kami* or spirit-like forces. Ritual practice involves sacred sites at national, local, and domestic levels where, respectively, the Emperor, priests, and family members make offerings and honour the forces of life and place. Sacred mountains and rivers, for example, as well as seasons of the year, often carry such significances.

Environmentalism – ecological movement

The twenty-first century has witnessed an intensified focus on longstanding interests in the natural environment, with ecological concerns assuming prime position in political concerns of world politics under the fear of global warming, and with the Covid-19 pandemic and vaccination programmes of 2021 reinforcing a scientific approach to world-processes of nature.

Scientific worldviews

From classical antiquity to modern times, human meaning-making has included studies of the world. However, from what is often called the Age of Enlightenment in the eighteenth century, and especially from the mid nineteenth century, empirical study of the world at large, largely separate from traditional religious teachings, has generated theories and practices that have transformed human existence. Life-span has increased for many in modern societies and anaesthesia, antibiotics, and vaccination have drastically reduced pain, suffering, and premature death. Engineering, too, has radically altered modes of transport and discovery, while town planning has fostered sanitary health and domestic dwelling. From astronomy to genetics, scientific methods have slowly generated an implicit worldview for millions in developed societies enhanced by institutions such as the British National Health Service.

Ancestral worldviews

Given the importance of kin group attachment for raising ongoing generations, it is not surprising that deceased ancestors should find a place in the narratives of past generations and even enter into the way the living sense themselves to be in contact with the dead, or to own devotional obligation to them. Here Confucianism, Judaism, and Mormonism have been singled out as examples.

Confucianism

Confucianism accords importance to dead relatives, whether recently deceased or as more distanced ancestors, and is influential in China and South Korea. This deeply social perspective fosters respect within forms of parent–child and teacher–pupil relationships amongst the living and frames them through attitudes to the dead. Often described as 'piety', such proper relationships sustain the good order of society. The question of the 'existence' of gods is largely irrelevant, while the use of domestic shrines is widespread as are periodic family-focused rites of respect to the ancestors.

Judaism

Ancient Judaism found community strength in tribal, patriarchal, prophetic, priestly, and regal-like figures embodying cultural responses to a divine revelation that spoke of a specially chosen people, covenant, and promised homeland that retains powerful resonance to this day in modern Israel. Judaism's attitude to these ancestral figures also played a profound role in new sects that contributed to emergent Christianity which, in turn, retained the high status of Jewish patriarchs and prophets while going on to venerate its own early founders, transforming the identity of many into being Saints, while identifying the Jewish Jesus as divine.

Mormonism

If Confucianism is 'Eastern', with Judaism and earliest Christianity being Middle-Eastern, many subsequent developments of Christianity found global, national, and local identity in churches and sects. Of all developments, none is more 'Western' and yet ancestrally focused than Mormonism. It exemplifies an ancestral worldview mirroring aspects of Ancient Israel's religious organisation. This Church of Jesus Christ of Latter-day Saints fosters extensive genealogical research on ancestors followed by highly ritualised temple work to foster their salvation.

Karmic worldviews

Widespread within India-derived groups often depicted as Hinduism, Buddhism, Jainism, and to some extent also Sikhism, this perspective focuses on the moral scheme of action and reaction or moral cause and effect driven by the notion of *karma*. This idea depicts a universe governed by a kind of impersonal scheme in which acts deemed good are rewarded positively but bad acts attract negative consequences. This scheme carries its own mythology and social organisation, notably in India's enduring caste system. Christianity, Islam, and many local traditions also embrace strong notions of rewards and punishments, sometimes complemented or transcended by notions of grace or supernatural, non-karmic, goodwill.

Prophetic – sectarian worldviews

Prophetic traditions are known in traditional Zoroastrianism, ancient Israel, and ensuing Judaism, Islam, and to some degree in Christianity where influential figures announce a message coming directly from some supernatural deity. Such prophets are often described sociologically as charismatic, attracting followers, and with ongoing generations often bringing more reasoned interpretations and commentaries to bear on the original announcements. Most of the world's sacred scriptures began as 'sayings' and went on to generate formal theologies and creeds sustained by hierarchies of scribes, scholars, and priests. This type is jointly described as 'sectarian' because prophetic-style leaders often generate new movements of protest in which pre-existing worldviews are re-fashioned, revitalised, or transformed, often through definitions of what is evil and how it may be overcome.

Mystical worldviews

In the history of religions, mysticism is often limited to distinctive individuals whose sense of transcendence and even union with the divine is deemed remarkable. Their heightened form of mystical union is probably but an intensified form of what many 'ordinary' people experience. This phenomenon can also be found in association with other worldviews, and has been increasingly considered in psychological studies of human mental states, including that of 'mindfulness'.

Ideological worldviews

Ideological worldviews embrace perspectives driven by specific theoretical sets of ideas posited on explicitly rational bases, and sometimes focused on a single issue. Though this general orientation to the world includes many potential groups and movements, only those of Communism and varieties of Secularism and Humanism are included here, due to their enormous effect on world history and today's international politics.

Communist ideology

Communism is the best-known ideology-driven worldview, having underpinned the Russian Revolution leading to the era of the United Soviet Socialist Republic (the former USSR), and with revolutions that engendered today's People's Republic of China, and of Cuba. Karl Marx and his theory of dialectical materialism, developed in different ways by other thinkers, notably Lenin, reckoned that there were principles or laws of social development rooted in ideas of social class, and differential power over workers by capitalist leaders. The goal of society was to remove these inequalities and redress the alienation of the worker from what was produced through capitalism.

Secular religion and secularism

Often following and transforming established patterns of religious practice yet denying any supernatural reference secular traditions have periodically emerged. Historically, the nineteenth century witnessed the creation of Secular Religion in France and some minor echoes currently exist in what has been devised in non-religious Sunday Assemblies in some western societies. Less group orientated, some public intellectuals, notably those driven by philosophical notions of rationality or of science, such as Richard Dawkins, are often seen to lead such science-driven worldviews that wish to eliminate or marginalise 'religious' agents. More broadly, secular-like concerns with Human Rights have driven many twentieth and twenty-first century issues in social policy and ethics.

Ludic worldviews

Ludic worldviews, developed from the Latin 'Ludo' – I play, seek to indicate outlooks in which playful emotional attitudes are advocated to provide a life-interest. While many aspects of human life are driven by ideas of play, the following examples of sport, internet gaming, narrative, film, and theatre have been singled out because of their widespread influence.

Sport

Sporting competition has long been important in human societies. Today, deep commitments are attached to teams and players, and to the ritual and art-forms of play in soccer, rugby, tennis, snooker, horse-racing, and many other sports. Notably celebrated and ritualised in the Olympic Games movement, the Ludic Worldview offers its own rationale for international relationships embracing the excellence of human bodies subjected to competition according to set rules. Cheating is reprehensible and being a 'good sport' is praised. In some ways, this competitive world reflects the ordinary world of rule-based living but in an intensified form.

Internet gaming

Internet activity devising imaginative worlds in which individuals engage, often through creating avatars of themselves, generates rule-controlled action engaging many millions of online players.

Narrative, Film, and Theatre

While narratives underlie practically all worldviews, they, too, are intensified in playful forms of making sense of the world in books, film-video, and theatre. These domains reveal not only human meaning-making capacity but also the devising of complex scenarios in which individuals and groups may play-out challenging situations. In film, these also provide occasions when the basic emotion of fear may be 'safely' experienced. All these highlight the radically basic nature of story to human existence and relationships.

Conclusion

Though presented here as distinct ideal types, worldviews sometimes morph from one to another over time. In any specific case, one significant aspect of a tradition may be best accounted for by one type, while other aspects may be better covered by one of the other types. In Christianity, for example, both prophetic and mystical streams have their own place; in Mormonism, strong ancestral features cover its sense of family, genealogical work, and temple ritual on behalf of the dead, while its origin lies in a strongly Prophetic tradition in terms of being a form of the Jewish-Christian perspective on divine revelation, sacred texts, and the role of individual prophets.

6 Natural worldview

Introduction

Natural Worldviews in this and Scientific Worldviews in the next chapter are strongly complementary. Beginning with how 'nature' and 'culture' are classified, this chapter discusses Animism, Shamanism, and Shinto, along with the innovative British practice of Natural Burial and then an account of the National Memorial Arboretum. All of these reveal a distinctive interest in the dynamic forces of nature through a diversity of cultural practices. Chapter seven then takes up ideas of ecology and environmentalism in a more direct relation to the radical significance of global warming and environmental disturbances that currently confront the whole of humanity and draw heavily on Scientific Worldviews.

Nature and Culture

One of the most extensive manifestations of the human drive for meaning is found in the ways humans classify the world when naming things and forming particular attitudes and behaviours towards them. In this sense, practically everything is 'cultural', including the notions of 'nature' and 'culture'. Generally speaking, what Britons call 'nature' differs from the perspectives of indigenous Australians, forest peoples of the African Congo, or various New Yorkers. A similar diversity would almost certainly apply to images and ideas of 'nature' held by British dentists, farmers, bankers, and many other groups, with sex differences, changing times, and circumstances also making an impact. As might then be expected, the following comparison of Lévi-Strauss and Descola, two anthropologists a generation apart, will aptly mark such shifting attitudes.

DOI: 10.4324/9781003242437-9

Nature versus culture: nature and culture

The distinction between 'nature' and 'culture' has long occupied European intellectual debates, not least as formulated by the French anthropologist Claude Lévi-Strauss (1963:99–104). When writing in the 1940s and 1950s, it seemed perfectly appropriate for him to say that 'culture ... relates to the specific differences between men and animals, thus leading to what has ever since been the classic antithesis between *nature* and *culture*' (Lévi-Strauss, [1958] 1968:356). Though this distinction was often rooted in the human capacity for tool making and language, times change, as with Philippe Descola's *Beyond Nature and Culture* (2005). This complex book links philosophical and anthropological ideas through some challenging ethnographic features. His reference to the former Jivaro headhunters, for example, discusses how 'manioc, the main foodstuff for the Jivaro and the most common plant in their environment, is reputed to suck in through its leaves the blood of those who brush by them'; moreover, incantations are sung to the plants that are, also raised as children who will be eaten (Descola, 2005:343). This vignette brings its own challenge to 'western' notions of 'nature' and 'culture' as well as to issues of identity and relationship. Since its publication in 2005, many advances in scientific knowledge of animals, plants, the earth, and their mutual interactions have inspired the complexity of nature–culture relationships, especially under the weight of climate change and its environmental peril for human populations.

Changing views now integrate the mutual existence of plants and animals within a growing framework of understanding human life that brings new issues to some traditional religious schemes. Notional distinctions between 'animal', 'plant', and 'humans' were, for example, vital within the biblical texts of Genesis and Leviticus for influencing both Jewish and Christian thought-worlds, especially over those deemed 'clean' or 'unclean' for sacrifice. Not only were unblemished animals used in Jewish sacrifice, but this rationale underlay the Christian image of Jesus, one believed to be the incarnate divine Son, depicted as the Lamb of God who takes away the sin of the world (John 1:29). Moreover, the Genesis (1:27) classification of humans – male and female created He them – also reflects a cultural classification of deity and humanity with consequences for today's world where gender-identity as a cultural category is much debated, and where divine 'revelation' sits alongside changing cultural attitudes to sexuality and gender as people of differing persuasions make their contradictory points. Just as sex, sexuality, and gender can be framed and interpreted by different worldviews, so too with the issue of 'forces' associated with 'nature' at large, a subject best discussed in terms of Animism.

Animism

Until the opening years of the twenty-first century, Animism was often considered a rather antique notion consigned to the early years of anthropological discussion in the late nineteenth century. But, again, things changed and, today, new theoretical insights emerge from innovative ethnographic studies. Two scholars, Tylor and Praet, help capture this interpretative shift.

E. B. Tylor (1832–1917)

We begin with the nineteenth-century birth of 'Animism' and the view that some peoples encounter the world as being full of energies and agents often described as spirits or forces, whether deemed relatively impersonal or personal. Historically, Sir Edward Burnett Tylor coined the term 'Animism' to describe this awareness of the dynamic forcefulness of the environment where trees, rivers, mountains, and other phenomena are treated as special, with respect, and perhaps even with awe. Key to this view is that humans are part and parcel of an interactive world possessing both visible and invisible elements.

Tylor, sometimes described as intellectualist to depict his rational approach, was one of the founders of British anthropology. Born of a Quaker industrialist family, he, like some other non-Anglicans, did not go to Oxford or Cambridge because until 1854, they expected students to agree with Church of England views on religion. Instead he went travelling and happened to meet a fellow Quaker who interested him in archaeology. This start, in Mexico, led him into 'anthropology', at a time when evolutionary theory was just beginning to take a distinctive scientific direction and appeal to a wide variety of thinkers, including Tylor. He saw that meaning-making was crucial to understanding human behaviour and in his influential book *Primitive Culture* clearly says that people are 'trying to get at the meaning of life' ([1871] 1958, vol. 1:22). His researches not only paid considerable attention to artefacts and material culture but also to the non-material domains of thought, dreams, and supernatural entities. Essentially, he dealt with the worldviews of peoples that are made up of material and non-material phenomena, but for present purposes, it is the latter that take precedence.

Tylor's own imagination underlies his interpretation of materials gathered from 'primitive' peoples, though when appropriate, he also included examples from contemporary Britain. His interest lay in the forces that many peoples spoke of when describing the nature of life, death, animals, plants, and special places, and certainly of human beings and the question of their destiny. Many social groups ponder the question of how a living person differs from a corpse, with notions of souls or spirits often used to account for that shift in identity. To create a category for studying this dynamic world, Tylor spoke of Animism. He would have preferred to speak of 'Spiritualism' but that term had already been adopted by the newly developing American group called Spiritualists associated with the Fox sisters in 1848. This Animism–Spiritualism distinction is a telling one for this chapter because the difference between them marks the difference between an essentially religious-supernatural category associated with religious worldviews on the one hand (Spiritualism), and a naturalistic-rational category more aligned with science on the other (Animism). That division was an interesting feature of the nineteenth century where some, especially higher social class groups, were becoming attracted to Spiritualism and supernatural phenomena while, at the same time, evolutionary theory was beginning to dominate the more scientific perspectives of others. One apt illustration can be drawn from a contemporary of Sir Edward Burnett Tylor, namely Sir Arthur Conan Doyle whose famous literary creation Sherlock Holmes, the rational, fact-driven, detective, contrasts with Sir Arthur's personal interest in Spiritualism, the para-normal, and the possibility of the living engaging with the dead through séances.

Tylor's Animism was, essentially, a theory of souls that also embraced the potential spirits of other animals, plants, and places: Animism was a theoretical account of forces of causation. Trying to 'think' as 'primitive' people think, he took the case of dreams and the way some idea of soul might explain how dreamers speak of taking journeys while asleep, and account for this by notions of their souls leaving their bodies and returning before they awoke. By implication, when a person was dead, it must be because their life-force or soul had left the body inert, gone for good. This then triggered thoughts of where the soul had gone, and by equal logic, where it had come from in the first place. By further implication, the living came to pay homage, including making sacrifices, to their absent dead, and over time those departed spirits developed a divine status that prompted devotion. Indeed Tylor's famous basic definition of religion was 'belief in spiritual beings', with Animism also serving as a 'groundwork for philosophy' ([1871] 1958, vol. 2:8,10). Such speculation, even though it drew from some available pragmatic descriptions of missionaries and travellers, was severely criticised by anthropologist Evans-Pritchard, who also criticised other speculative theories of religion (1965).

However, not all of Tylor's work circled around speculation on 'primitive' thought. He also stressed the significance of ritual behaviour, something he depicted as 'the gesture-language of theology', through whose 'expressive and symbolic performances' people reckoned to engage with supernatural agents while seeking to influence them to be generous to humans ([1871]

1958, vol. 2:448). Tylor's outlook typified an emergent rationalist and scientific study of religion that firmly set supernaturally aligned practices and thoughts of 'primitive' peoples within a natural category open to anthropological analysis. One historian who has also explored issues of Spiritualism, especially in the USA, has been appreciative of Tylor's work and how his interest in Animism fed into the growing discipline of anthropology (Taves, 1999).

Istvan Praet

Moving to the twenty-first century, one of numerous anthropologists who challenge how we perceive and classify things and agencies around us is Istvan Praet. His *Animism and the Question of Life* positively acknowledges 'Animism' as a 'doctrine of universal vitality', noting Tylor's 'distinctly biological definition of life' and his 'distinctly biological definition of humanity' (Praet 2014:2). While appreciating that perspective, Praet criticises today's excessive emphasis on biology as such and seeks to bring a more cultural frame to life-issues. Crucially for this worldviews book, he wants to take Animism 'out of religious studies' and give it a wider framework (2014:4), and by setting his comments in a 'worldview' perspective this will help achieve that goal. Praet shows how philosophical issues sit alongside social scientific concerns with 'life' at large, and certainly provides a distinctive way of appreciating that today is 'an age of environmental crisis', in which 'Animism is no longer seen as backward but as praiseworthy and sensible' (2014:3). He shows how anthropological ethnographies are driven by how different groups classify things, whether as 'dead' or 'alive' or even as something else. And it is that 'something else' that may sound strange to many, for by focussing on 'life' he isn't just wanting some appreciation of a life-force or energy 'in nature', but of the way humans approach things, categorise, and respond to them. He juggles with his readers' ordinary conceptions and tries to get people to see things differently, and in the process to acknowledge, how we 'feel' things too.

'Life' is a shape

'Life' is a crucial question for Praet. This is clear when he announces that his 'proposal is to reformulate the question of life in a manner that completely shakes off the premises of the biological framework wherein it had gotten entrapped' (2014:8). So 'life' is not the prime domain of biology, it is a much wider experience. 'Instead of focussing on the modern biological conception of life, we have to study life as a positional quality' (2014:93). This means that he invites us to shake-up our ordinary 'western' dichotomy

between 'life' and 'death', and to understand that 'humanity requires perpetual effort' (2014:34, 101, 199). At first, this may sound strange, but his
goal is to think of human identity in terms of a certain dynamism underlying
life. This becomes clearer when he analyses cultural energy and a person's
participation in society in terms of turning a *human* (he uses the lower case
'h') into a *Human* (with the upper-case 'H'). This challenges many ordinary
'western' ways of thinking about identity. He develops his way of thinking
still further and speaks of the 'shape' of a person's existence at any one
time, and of a person's capacity to 'shape-shift'. Praet is, here, trying to
explain an unfamiliar worldview to his readers. This includes a recognition
that 'Humanity requires a perpetual effort' (2014:101): note the capital H
in this sentence which highlights the notion that living and contributing to
one's community and to oneself as a member requires effort and input that
also enhances identity. We might, for example, adapt it and say that being
a Student (capital S) requires perpetual effort while being a student (lower
case 's') might not involve much effortful commitment. These issues of
energy and classification run across Praet's work, including issues of sickness so that, 'becoming ill implies that one is no longer Alive' but in a sense
'Dead', which means that those who cure them have to become like them in
some respects 'they are obliged to die temporarily', and this might involve
taking hallucinogens or 'eating anti-food' (2014:102). A similar idea takes
the form of 'the wounded healer', the thought that someone who has suf-
fered is better able to empathise and relate to those who suffer (Davies,
2002:147).

So, although Praet and Tylor deal with Animism in different ways, they
raise prime questions on how human beings classify and interact with their
environment. One closely related area of research is that of Shamanism and
its expression of dynamic energies that are often personalised, personified,
and put to good community ends.

Shamanism

Theoretical notions of Shamanism involve persons who, through ritual performances, are credited with the capacity to enter into alliances with spirits
or supernatural agents. Today, shamans are found across the world in individuals able to heal or to assist with community difficulties by drawing on
supernatural-style resources. What is often described as Neo-Shamanism
is also practised by contemporary western groups in a kind of mirroring of
'traditional' Shamanism, and frequently employ musical rhythm in drumming and chanting to enter a trance state. This form of transcendence gives
the sense of experiencing something beyond the everyday life-world. As
with many practices that move from one society to another, some are due

to migrant practitioners who make it possible for new groups to appropriate what others have long found of value, but sometimes scholars may also trigger interest in ancient ways, and one such was Eliade.

Mircea Eliade (1907–1986)

Eliade, a highly influential scholar in the history of religions' – the term covering the way many European scholars study comparative religion – was foundational for modern interest in Shamanism, as also for Yoga as a later chapter on Mystical Worldview shows. As one of the most prolific of twentieth century scholars of religion his work ranges far and wide and is not always easy to categorise. Still, regarding Shamanism he spoke of a phenomenon that 'defends life, health, fertility, the world of "light" against death, diseases, sterility, disaster, and the world of "darkness"', while also being 'being able to contribute decisively to the knowledge of death' (1964:509). In spotlighting the idea of flaws in the nature of existence and of the shaman as fostering forms of resolution this echoes notions of 'evil' and 'salvation' as a coping strategy. If 'salvation' is deemed too loaded a 'religious term', it could easily be replaced by deliverance or resolution.

Though Eliade's text has been much criticised since first published in French in 1951 it remains a historical classic. Its Foreword offers a brief account of different methods of study, noting his preferred notion of the 'history of religions' whose 'mission is to integrate the results of ethnology, psychology, and sociology', and the idea of 'hierophany', a term covering the manifestation of the sacred whether in a tree, prophet, or other feature. Eliade usefully observes that 'Shamanism is precisely one of the archaic techniques of ecstasy – at once mysticism, magic and "religion" in the broadest sense of the term' ([1951] 1964:xiii, xix). In some ways, his general depiction pinpoints a widespread type of human behaviour that singles out a person within a community who is reckoned to have some special power to engage with spirits for the advantage of the home community. Here is found healing and the means of coping with misfortune. Many later studies have given concrete cases whether from Northern Siberia, often argued as the source of the notion shaman, or from indigenous North and South America, contemporary South Korea, and Japan. Neo-Shamanism is a term often used today for some contemporary western practices sometimes allied with Pagan or New-Age forms of spirituality with its focus on drumming, dancing, altered states of consciousness, and a sense of engaging with forces of nature and supernatural domains (Jakobsen, 1999:147–207). For odd historical reasons of academic fashion, it has not been customary in the UK to speak of 'Shamanism' in Africa despite the incidence of some possession-like practices. In all these discussions, care is needed over the terms 'natural' and 'supernatural' since each may mean something different to researchers and practitioners and their respective perception of the world around them. Similarly, though Neo-Shamanism is a modern invention pursued as a personal interest and not a more established part of a traditional community, some might see both as drawing upon what Eliade would take to be a natural propensity of humans to engage with a transcendent focus. Some caution also surrounds the next case where Shinto is brought under the general category of Natural Religion.

Shinto

One reason for placing Shinto in the same worldview category of Natural Religion alongside Animism is because some scholars, notably Rein Raud, acknowledge how some studies of 'religion' align Shinto with 'an animist worldview' (2021:213). Another reason is to highlight the sheer complexity of human social-cultural life where attitudes towards nature as a spirit-pervaded environment have combined with political power through mythical narratives and ritual, whether at imperial palaces or in ordinary domestic settings. In Shinto, that combination seems to have formed a worldview of its own. Moreover, Raud emphasises how Shinto, as a major phenomenon in Japan, manifests an 'absence of distinct borders between the sacred and the profane', with the 'whole universe' being 'alive, filled with spiritual energy', with some locations manifesting 'a higher concentration of that energy than others', something that 'elicits respect and admiration' from people, bringing them into some 'state of betweenness ' in terms of different locales (2021:214). These factors prompt two significant themes, ritual purity and the power of words.

Ritual Purity is a complex idea because it is both a theoretical concept and a bundle of practical behaviours or, in technical terms, it has 'etic' and 'emic' features. The term 'etic' refers to formal, abstract, scholarly interpretations of behaviours, while 'emic' explanations are those provided by local people commenting on their own actions. These expressions often occur in studies of religious activity. Sometimes etic interpretations closely mirror emic accounts, but sometimes they are quite different, depending on the kind of theories used to interpret behaviour. Whatever is the case, the idea of ritual purity is often complex and always needs contextual analysis. Raud's approach is more descriptive than interpretative but provides one clue to ideas of purity when noting that – 'death is one of the most active sources of pollution and the death of the emperor pollutes more than that of the ordinary individual'; that in ancient times, the Japanese 'moved their capital to a new site every time an emperor died', and that periodically some Shinto shrines were 'dismantled and then rebuilt' on the same plan, 'from new and pure materials' (2021:216). Visits to shrines involve hand and mouth washing and as, over time, Buddhism established itself in Japan death came under its ritual practices. In this Japanese context, pollution is set in opposition to life or vitality factors. Just as the shrines intensify the dynamic spiritual energy of the world open for devotees to access, so death intensifies negative aspects of existence. But 'pollution' also carries some longer association with some trades, as with leather workers and those dealing with dead animals that aptly symbolise death. Moreover, wider 'feelings of guilt and traces of wrongdoing are a kind of pollution that gathers in the mind', only to be resolved through ritual activity (2021:16). Here it would seem that acts disordering social life and duty count as impure just as death itself mars social existence, especially in the person of the emperor.

It is as though the human drive for meaning, especially in its ordering of society, needs re-shaping when spoiled by misbehaviour and death: the mind and its overloaded, negative, memories can be recomposed. And here 'words' help play a part when the vitality of spirit-flooded phenomena requires ritual sustenance. When it comes to what Raud depicts as 'the spirit of words' or the 'magical power, or "spirit" of ... words', he thinks of 'spells and incantations', touching 'poetry and song': moreover extended narratives also play a significant role in what are origin-myths depicting the emergence of *kami* – spirits that emerged out of chaos with an ensuing creation of the Japanese islands (2021:217).

The *kami* influence people's environment even though their 'active' nature may not be conceived in terms of the personal agency of some divinity. This may be difficult for devotees of traditions whose forces are often depicted as 'personal' agents, e.g. God, Christ, Allah, or ancestors who 'know', 'see', record, and have direct intentions. Still, at Shinto sites, priests and people make offerings and honour the forces of life in mountains, rivers, and seasons of the year. When Victoria Urubshurow's comparative study of religions discusses Shinto and its 'Ultimate Principle', she engages with the 'mysterious-nature-life-creative energy' subsumed in the notion of *kami*, and divides this 'Mysterious creative Life Energy of Nature' between 'Nature kami' and Mythic kami, the former embracing some trees, food, growth, wild animals, mountains with aligned pilgrimages, geological features, crossroads and houses (2008:323). Amidst the Mythic Kami, she pinpoints the figure of Amaterasu associated with the sun, the clan kami of Japanese families, including the family of the Emperor reckoned to be descended from the sun. The intricate political–historical and mythological dynamics of Japan's cultural worldview that had long pivoted around the imperial family and its ritual-cultural traditions culminated in the Emperor Hirohito (1901–1989) declaring on 1st January 1946 that he was not divine: a major consequence of Japan's defeat in the

Second World War. Still, the ritual–cultural, if not political, nature of the imperial office continues in modified forms as when Naruhito succeeded his father to the Chrysanthemum Throne in May 2019 accompanied with some traditional Shinto rites being televised. This case aptly demonstrates the integrated complexity of perceived forces of nature, state authority, and dramatic political change, not least as post-war Japan arose as a major international economy whose worldview embraces yet transforms many of its antecedent perspectives.

Natural Burial and National Memorial Arboretum, UK

Two rather different contexts where distinctive aspects of a natural worldview provide a frame for cultural events can be found in, first, the hundreds of natural or woodland burial sites located across Great Britain and, second, in the single large site of the National Memorial Arboretum in the English Midlands near the city of Lichfield. Together, these serve well to focus on how 'nature' comes to be symbolised in and through trees as a framework for death, funerals, and grand scale memorials.

Natural Burial

From the mid-1990s, the British began to bury corpses in what are variously called natural, woodland, ecological, or green burials, each name carrying its own significance. Research has shown how people involved in such sites, and there are more than three hundred across the UK, speak of 'nature' as a context attracting their interest as far as their own place of burial is concerned. Some specifically express the desire to 'give something back' to the earth and contribute to places for future generations to visit. Some also see these locations in terms of fulfilling their cycle of life (Davies and Rumble, 2012). These sentiments express something of the 'natural' nature of death and not its 'unnatural' nature as depicted in some traditional religious approaches. Many of these sites do not allow for traditional stone headstones, nor coffins that are not easily biodegradable. Records are kept of where corpses are buried, but over time, the actual visible grave becomes submerged by plant life.

National Memorial Arboretum

In 2001, the National Memorial Arboretum was opened by the Duchess of Kent, on some 150 acres of land at Alrewas near Lichfield. It contains an enormous central memorial located on an artificially built hill, holding names of people killed since the Second World War in the military forces.

Many other memorials represent hundreds of British military and civilian organisations that, together, provide many windows onto the complex diversity of British cultural life. This remarkable place was established by Commander David Childs of the Royal Navy and he has published his own account of its origin (2008). The key point for our purpose is that trees of very many kinds serve as the natural frame for these many memorials (Guidebook, 2017). While 'Arboretum' is a widely recognised term for a collection of trees, and Britain has many of these, this one is unique in its national scale and focus on memorialising many groups. It is also a place of varied ritual-symbolic activity across the year, both in formal memorial ceremonies and in many informal, small group, and personal events.

The anthropologist Claude Lévi-Strauss once spoke of certain things as being 'good to think' (1962:89). He meant that some issues, especially if they are more abstract, are more easily grasped if symbolised in certain objects, or in the interplay of plants and animals. The 'green belt' around a town, rain forests, or parks and gardens, can all provide examples of how we think of ourselves in relation to 'nature'. Note how this was once the case with circuses, zoos, and their animals – though now we see 'wild' animals as cruelly kept in both contexts, just as 'intelligent' dolphins and whales ought not to be held 'captive' for our amusement. It is interesting that trees have become particularly singled out as symbolic phenomena as ecological–environmental concerns have grown in significance in the twenty-first century. Just as certain trees have played significant roles in the narrative accounts of many traditional religious traditions so they are emerging in contemporary narratives of the environment. Humans often find it easy to experience an affinity with some kinds of trees. Size, capacity for lasting centuries beyond human life-span, as well as providing shade and fruit, all add to their appeal. Today their importance lies in helping to form narratives allowing intricate scientific issues to be presented in much simpler story-form, and that is vital for 'thinking through' contemporary ecological–environmental issues.

Conclusion

This chapter has linked aspects of culture and approaches to the study of religion that have not been brought together before. Yet, Animism, Shamanism, and Shinto, as well as the practice of natural burial, and the remarkable National Memorial Arboretum as an environment of remembrance and hope for future peace, demonstrate the dynamic power that many people sense in the world around them.

7 Scientific worldview

Introduction

To engage briefly with the idea of Scientific Worldviews inevitably demands sharp focus because 'science' covers the spectrum of knowledge from astronomy to zoology and embraces the radical transformation in approaches to knowledge from the seventeenth century onwards. As theories concerning the nature of the world emerged alongside empirical fields of detailed study, research-driven experimentation largely replaced reception of mythological, theological, and more speculative philosophical ways of thinking. The key difference between the provisional nature of scientific discovery and the certainties of revealed truths leads some to a sharp divide between 'science' and 'religion', while others adopt them in parallel or as complementary ways of engaging with the world. Still, scientific discoveries underlie technology and the fabric of contemporary society in ways that foster a scientific worldview. Moreover, the global climate crisis and the 2021 Covid-19 viral pandemic have brought science to the absolute centre of political and cultural life, and especially in response to death and survival.

Crises and science

This combination of pandemic and global warming crises is incredibly significant because it links two dimensions of scientific theory. One belongs to astronomy, physics, and the distant future of an uninhabitable earth and self-destructing universe, and the other to the shorter-term fields of ecological–biological–medical science and the immediate survival and flourishing of people. This tends to mean that the notion of a 'scientific worldview' operates at different levels of human interest with time-scales that are either immediately relevant or unimaginably distant. This is where the Covid-19 pandemic has played a curious role, not only in the immediacy of personal and family

DOI: 10.4324/9781003242437-10

death and survival but as an intensifier of the ecological and environmental urgency of global warming that, in some symbolic fashion, heralds the very much longer-term viability of the earth in sustaining human life. These issues not only mark the important role of scientific institutions but of how their findings reach a mass population. While research institutes, universities, expert academies, and research publications generate, test, and apply theories whether in engineering, policing, or healthcare, many aspects of science remain distant abstractions for most people, leaving considerable need to bridge the gap. This includes the need for specific scientists to embody 'scientific knowledge' and to create attractive narratives for non-scientific groups of the public. Historically, this has been partly the case with Charles Darwin (1809–1882) and Albert Einstein (1879–1955), and continues in the UK today by only a handful of scientists such as the biologist Desmond Morris (born 1928), primatologist Jane Goodall (born 1934), astronomer-physicist Brian Cox (born 1968), and Suzanne Simard who is discussed below for her work on trees. Their information-driven narratives, opinions, and stories are highly significant because narrative is crucial for communicating core values at a public level. Stories communicate in ways that theories find difficult. Even so, some aspects of an ever emerging scientific set of worldviews are essentially complex and far from easy to communicate, as with the rapidly developing field of cognitive and brain science embracing issues of consciousness, selfhood, and the creative interface of brain, body, and environment.

Moreover, the impact of a scientific worldview cannot be separated from ethical issues for it raises ethical considerations whether in terms of atomic explosion, genetic manipulation, and – now – especially in terms of ecology and environmentalism. As such it is also inextricably linked to political decision-making at national and global levels. No worldview exists in isolation from others, and the scientific worldview is and will remain of paramount significance, both for dealing with climate change and the future impact of pandemics. What is also of crucial significance for worldviews and religious studies is that considerable work remains to be done in interpreting scientific methods and findings within the theological–philosophical realms of major religious traditions. The 'science and religion' arena remains significant for many world contexts especially when involving a clash of worldviews or when conspiracy theories pervade social and other media and contradict scientific understanding, as over the Covid-19 pandemic period.

National welfare, religion, and secularity

One major aspect of the scientific worldview affecting many people lies in medical-healthcare provision. Recent research comparing Sweden and the USA has found strong evidence to suggest that 'the strongest predictor of the degree of religiosity versus secularism' lies in the 'proportion of Gross National Product' spent on 'welfare functions including health insurance, schools, pensions, … the more governments spend on welfare, the less religious are their populations' (Granqvist, 2020:304). To a degree, this informative material would also seem applicable to the UK and the fact that most British citizens are embedded in the health care provision of the National Health Service (NHS) which combines medical science with social welfare and ethical concerns, all in terms of government funding and political decision-making. The widespread existence of local medical centres and regional and national hospitals provides an arena in which scientific and clinical research reaches individuals whose personal knowledge of science is minimal. From its political origin in 1946–1948, this NHS grew to embrace increasing numbers of ailments and concerns and now embraces people from the beginning of pregnancy through to their death (Davies, 2017:98–103).

The Covid-19 pandemic of 2021 brought this entire service to the absolute centre of public attention with the idea of preserving life becoming increasingly clear as a core cultural value driven by the NHS. This was in some key respects ritualised in public 'clapping' for the NHS workers as well as in thousands of small and large signs supporting and thanking the NHS for its work (Davies, 2022). At the same time, the dramatically speedy work of scientists in producing vaccines to protect against viral death brought the very idea of expertise in science to the forefront of public life, frequently represented by the UK's chief medical officers standing alongside the prime minister and other key politicians during televised presentations that took on their own ritual-symbolic character. Vaccines and vaccination emerged as symbols of hope against untimely death. Similarly, the very term 'professor' seemed to rise to the surface as a mark of respect, and, in some ways, an expression, of the validity of experts. This was something quite different from the 'celebrity' status of entertainment people whose only claim to fame was 'being' famous in the media for no apparent reason other than their physical appearance or displayed individuality.

Natural complexity and consilience

Quite different from televised presentation of medical statistics on infection, hospitalisation and death rates during the Covid-19 crisis period, the following scientists and thinkers have been chosen to cover several centuries of research revealing the complexity of the natural world in its attraction, fascination, and even ethical concerns. Each provides a valuable element that feeds into a scientific worldview of considerable application for Worldview Religious Studies.

Von Humbolt, Whewell: 'Scientist' and Consilience

Alexander Von Humbolt (1769–1859), a remarkable German scholar and explorer, researched many fields. His sense of engaged knowledge invited his readers' imagination to participate in what is found in nature, an attitude that is now particularly appropriate for the early twenty-first century. Jackson and Walls documented how he merged the ideas and materials of 'geology, physiology ... geophysics ... movements of plant and animal species, vegetation patterns, anthropology ...weather, climate... and more', to create something analogous to today's 'earth systems science'. They also mention his links with the William Whewell (1794–1866), an Anglican priest, scholar, and Master of Trinity College Cambridge who invented the word 'scientist' and the notion of 'consilience' – 'the process by which two or more previously separate streams of research merge to make a new, transformed, whole'; it is precisely such consilience that is demanded for today's multi-disciplinary challenge of climate change that brings ethical issues alongside scientific concerns (Jackson and Walls, 2014:12).

Fish, octopus, and trees

Many elements are needed to feed such consilience-based processes and this will be enhanced if and when public interest is triggered. Of many possible studies, only three are pinpointed here – fish, octopus, and trees – chosen for their capacity to foster curiosity in a natural worldview.

Scientific studies transform many popular misconceptions, not least ideas of fish, where research has revealed significant levels of 'awareness and cognitive skills', including their 'sentience – the capacity to feel, to suffer pain, to experience joy', issues that furnish 'the bedrock of ethics'. Balcombe's work leads to seeing that 'fishes are beginning to take their place in the moral community. In parts of Europe it is now unlawful to keep a goldfish – a naturally social animal who can live for decades – alone in a barren fishbowl' (Balcombe, 2016:233). Moreover, experiments report depression and stress amongst some fish that was overcome by drugs (Valium and Prozac), and even by an artificial fish that moved and served as a 'comfort' to some fishes placed in stressful contexts (2016:92–3).

As for the octopus, Godfrey-Smith's research provides its own fascinating account of consciousness and sentience. He discusses how philosophers and others have pondered these complex issues through the human phenomenon of inner-speech and people's search for the self. When turning to octopuses, he pursues the notion of 'sentience' as 'not just bathing in living activity' but also involving 'pain as a basic and widespread form of subjective experience, one present in animals with very different brains from ours' (2016:95–6). Here, again, ethical issues arise on catching, killing, and eating octopus and squid, often on restaurant menus as *calamari*. Similarly, his account of 'friendliness', and the 'active engagement' as cuttlefish making 'contact with a foreign being' (a human), raises issues of relationships across species that pass into a degree of empathy. Such responsive feeling is captured in his depiction of the rapid and myriad colour shifts and physical changes cephalopods often make, leading him to speak of them as seemingly 'immensely *expressive* animals, animals with a lot to say' (2016:108, emphasis original). His account of the octopus as possessing a different kind of 'embodiment' from humans is also challenging: 'The octopus is suffused with nervousness: the body is not a separate thing that is controlled by the brain or nervous system' (2016:75). Such knowledge of 'other' animals prompts our own self-knowledge, and perhaps nowhere has this been more extensively appreciated than in studies of trees.

As the twenty-first century advanced, trees have assumed an ever increasing significance not only for global warming, tropical rain forests, deforestation, and the politics of climate control but also in scientific research that carries the capability of reframing human views of the world. Many cameo studies highlight the issues involved. Peter Wohlleben, for example, considers cases such as the oldest spruce in Sweden, now carbon dated as being 9,550 years old – something that offers a time-frame for human old-age, or of tree roots as the 'brain of the tree', that re-sets human self-reflection on 'consciousness'. He cites research on 'the opinion that brain-like structures can be found at root tips, with 'numerous systems and molecules similar to those found in animals' (2017:81, 83.) Key to these perspectives have been highly original and influential papers by Suzanne Simard and others (Simard et al., 1997, Beiler et al., 2010) reporting on how trees can share nutriment across root systems and engage in a kind of 'wood-wide web' of communications both underground and through pheromones passed by the wind. Moreover, 'Leaf tissue' may 'send out electrical signals, just as human tissue does when it is hurt' (Wohlleben, 2017:80). This research is an eye-opener for those from cultures where plants are just plants, or trees just trees, and where we see brains as setting humans so superbly apart. Almost as a key text for a natural worldview that evokes a human response, Dr Suzanne Simard writes in the postscript for Wohlleben's book, telling of her own doctoral work that began only in 1992.

> I discovered that the vast belowground mycelial network was a bustling community of mycorrhizal fungal species. These fungi are mutualistic.

They connect the trees with the soil in a market exchange of carbon and nutrients ... in a busy, cooperative Internet. ... I could see, using mass spectometers and scintillation counters, carbon being transmitted back and forth between the trees, like neurotransmitters firing in our own neural networks. The trees were communicating through the web!

(2017:248–89)

In such studies, many cultural assumptions are challenged through the work of science to feed and foster an emergent 'natural worldview'. This is related to the previous chapter's account of woodland burial, to which could be added increasing research on how plants help human integrity and happiness (Gillis and Gatersleben, 2015). These and other studies reflect the need for consilience in generating human responses as a natural species interacting with all other systems for a degree of optimal survival and flourishing.

Narratives of natural systems

Such new accounts of nature, following the nineteenth century establishment of Evolution, provide a powerful depiction of physical existence, and neither their significance nor rapidity of rise to dominance of this natural worldview can be underestimated. Just how this knowledge can be conveyed to advantage stands as a contemporary challenge. Suzanne Simard's research is one beacon of inspiring knowledge that sets science in a biography of discovery of interest to people at large and is enormously fruitful for a science-informed natural worldview. Similarly, the accidental meeting of earth scientist James Lovelock with novelist William Golding led to the latter suggesting the word 'Gaia' – a Greek name of an earth goddess – as a name for Lovelock's scientific vision of the multiple processes governing the earth's self-regulation: 'The theory is that, since it began, life has worked to modify its environment' (Lovelock, 2019:12–3). If not in Gaia theory as such, strong scientific evidence now acknowledges humanity's effect on climate change and is bringing about a paradigm shift as diverse scientific ideas mutually align in an emergent worldview, and it is this that we acknowledge as the 'natural worldview'. As with all worldviews, this too benefits from embodiment in influential individuals who can stimulate popular engagement, as with James Lovelock, Suzanne Simard, and highly influential media individuals such as Sir David Attenborough (2021) as well as the previous US vice-president Al Gore (2006).

Environmentalism, ecology, politics – a new grand narrative

Only in the 2020s has the critical nature of global warming and the vital complexity of what is, essentially, a natural worldview based on scientific research become a high priority of politicians with international agreements on climate change assuming worldwide–political–ethical–social–cultural terms. This is now coming to provide one grand narrative of contemporary life. The radical problems in global warming and other deleterious impacts upon world ecology can be pinpointed as radical constraints upon meaning-making.

In terms of this book, such 'radical constraints' constitute an 'evil' factor militating against human survival and flourishing. This is an important issue in that the idea of 'evil' has usually been restricted to theological or philosophical discussions, but it has also been studied as part of plausibility within the sociology of knowledge, as well as for anthropological ideas of evil (Davies, 1984:29–61). This approach brings the issue of natural and, indeed, of scientific worldview issues into wider human concerns of existence. In this sense, 'evil' is a concept perfectly extendable to embrace issues of survival. This also means that the international and national strategies of coping with disaster are not far from the notion of salvation.

One of the key texts of this emergent grand narrative of disaster and survival, or of 'evil' and 'salvation' as it might be framed in terms of the sociology of knowledge, lies in the 2015 *Paris Agreement* of the United Nations, of which this is but an extract:

> Acknowledging that climate change is a common concern of humankind, Parties should, when taking action to address climate change, respect, promote and consider their respective obligations on human rights, the right to health, the rights of indigenous peoples, local communities, migrants, children, persons with disabilities and people in vulnerable situations and the right to development, as well as gender equality, empowerment of women and intergenerational equity.

It also recognises 'the importance of the conservation and enhancement, as appropriate, of sinks and reservoirs of the greenhouse gases' and notes 'the importance of ensuring the integrity of all ecosystems, including oceans, and the protection of biodiversity, recognized by some cultures as Mother Earth, and noting the importance for some of the concepts of "climate justice", when taking action to address climate change'. It also affirms 'the importance of education, training, public awareness, public participation, public access to information and cooperation at all levels on the matters addressed in this Agreement'. The agreement inevitably recognised 'the importance of the engagements of all levels of government and various actors, in accordance with respective national legislations of Parties, in addressing climate change', as well as the fact that 'sustainable lifestyles and sustainable patterns of consumption and production, with developed country Parties taking the lead, play an important role in addressing climate change'.

Against that background, many informal eco-environmental groups have emerged in protest against environmental abuse and commercial profit-motives taking preference over conservation. The activity of the teenage Swede Greta Thunberg has made a worldwide impact, addressing the United Nations Climate Change Conference of 2017 and with her own book of speeches (2019). Her protest extended into 'School Strike for Climate' (SS4C), while other groups appeared around 2018, including Extinction Rebellion, a non-violent movement often adopting civil disobedience as its method of publicity and protest, these resonate a little with the prophetic-sectarian type of worldview in a later chapter. One background factor that links Greta Thunberg – as a Swedish citizen – with 'nature' and 'science', and even with the UK, lies with the great Swedish Professor Linnaeus of Uppsala University already discussed for his classification of plants. When he died, his remarkable collection of some 19,000 plant specimens, mostly dried, 3,000 books and other items came up for sale, and it was offered to the famous British Botanist Joseph Banks. With the help of rich patrons, he purchased it despite interests from Catherine the Great of Russia and King Gustav of Sweden who had placed a ban on its export but – fortunately for Banks and the UK, the ship had already sailed! (Wulf, 2008:222–3). These historical cameos are useful in understanding the background for British and other interests in gardens and parks that have helped prepare a way of thinking about 'nature' for many urban dwellers, as well as for new research on the benefit of plants for human wellbeing indoors as well as out.

Conclusion

The scientific method, grounded in theoretical hypotheses, empirical experimentation, the provisional acceptance of results, and the anticipation of ongoing insights, has radically changed ways of life and thought in the developed and developing worlds. The discovery of anaesthetics, antibiotics, vaccines, genetic manipulation, palliative care, and many other processes has transformed aspects of childbirth, infant mortality rates, sickness, pain, suffering, and even of dying. In these contexts, 'science' helps form part of many people's worldviews while being quite central to how some scientists and their institutions function. What is obvious is that ethical considerations frequently parallel scientific discovery, especially in terms of application, as was the case with the atom bomb and continues in chemical warfare, and this is now increasingly evident in terms of global warming which can, in a broad sense, be seen as an 'evil', or a severe constraint upon human survival. This reflects the meaning-making and the way humans have not only sought meaning in the world but also pinpointed certain problematic areas that seem to frustrate meaningfulness. Many religious worldviews have been good at intensifying such negative elements and setting about resolving them in processes of salvation. Scientific worldviews reset issues of 'evil' and 'salvation'.

8   Ancestral worldview

Introduction

Just as the power of narrative links scientific ideas with their famed discoverers, so too with ancestral worldviews. Ancestors frame how some groups think of themselves, often using myths, storytelling, and literary narratives alongside celebratory, memorial, and ritual-symbolic practices. Of many possible examples, we bring some mid-range theories of attachment, group identity, and destiny to interpretations of ancient Judaism, Confucian life, and Mormon practices of salvation.

Attachment theory, narrative, and ancestors

One valuable approach to Ancestral Worldviews is through attachment theory, a major psychological–sociological theoretical perspective that underlies ideas of child development and patterns of attachment children form with parental figures. Attachment theory has also been applied to various therapeutic situations, including bereavement and grief (Dallos, 2004, Loetz et al., 2013). More recently it has also been applied to religious contexts, attachment to God, spirituality at large, and to the Bible as a grand narrative for faith (Keller and Strieb, 2013, Knabb and Emerson, 2013, Granqvist, 2020). Applying ideas of attachment to ancestral figures and the myths, texts, and doctrines portraying them, and also recalling the ritual-symbolic events supporting them, we see that what is easily downplayed as 'ancestor worship' comes more in line with more established 'world' religions. The theoretical linking of attachment theory to religion has been significantly spearheaded by Pehr Granqvist in the idea of 'an attachment-religion connection' (2021:45). Although he has conducted experiments and gathered the results of many other experimental projects to show how issues of attachment to an idea of God accompanies some people in situations of crisis and distress, suggesting that God be thought of as a 'safe

DOI: 10.4324/9781003242437-11

haven' and 'secure base', he retains a degree of caution in thinking of 'God' as being just like a 'person' to whom attachment is feasible and often found (2021:54–5). Interestingly, he speaks of a 'fuzzy boundary' around God as attachment figure, but thinks there is much to explore in this idea, and he invokes the wider philosophical idea of family resemblances between things (2021:64), a perspective echoing the idea of deutero or second-order concepts mentioned in the Introduction to this book.

Certainly, the social nature of human beings takes shape through initial infant dependency on adults and ongoing community support. Born relatively unformed and taking years to mature, people have extensive opportunity to learn community stories that contribute to their own sense of identity while also enhancing the status of ancestors, much as in Mol's theory of the sacralisation of identity.

For much of humanity's evolution close kin contexts have provided the basic social environment of survival where patterns of ancestral descent and alliance frequently involve schemes of authority and respect aligned with forms of inheritance of land, property, or reputation. Ancestors matter, as do duty and obligation to and from them. While respect is obvious between older and younger living members of a group, but just because someone is 'dead' does not mean that they cease to be ascribed agency and status by the living. In very informal ways, some have reflected on how they sometimes identify aspects of their own appearance and behaviour with those of deceased parents in moments of everyday life (Young, 2002). Funerary rites, and sometimes other rites too, are occasions when descent is noted and obligations marked between past and present members of a kin group. Issues of identity are also often associated with funerals as in traditional Indian cremation when it was the duty of the eldest son to crack the skull of the parent on the pyre to allow the life-force to be set free for its onward journey (Parry, 1994). Within British societies someone's Last Will and Testament brings their wishes to bear upon their descendants. Yet other aspects of the agency of the dead occur in dreams, when the dead 'appear' to us, or seem to communicate with us.

Ancestral cases

It is highly likely that the ceremonial and cultural life of many pre-historic societies possessed ancestral dimensions, probably associated with forms of burial, recalling the adventures of the dead and their ongoing relationships with the living. Of many potential cases of ancestral worldviews just three are sketched here, drawn from Ancient Israel, contemporary Mormonism, and Confucianism, embracing ancient and modern times as well as a wide social–geographical range of peoples.

Judaism

Ancestors played a dramatically significant role in Judaism, a group believed to have been addressed by God and called to be a divinely chosen people destined for their own promised land. This remains a profound religious dispute in Israeli and Palestinian geopolitics where Jewish, Muslim, and varieties of Christians claim rights of possession of sacred places and physical territory. The importance of ancestors in ancient Judaism has been captured through the methods of archaeology, anthropology, and textual analysis, focused on funerary rites. Suriano, for example, develops the idea of 'functional immortality' to describe how the living treated their dead in Iron Age Judah (2018:6, 249–52). He proposes that ancestral 'souls' carried significance for as long as living descendants cared for them, and that they were not 'eternal' in the sense often associated with classical antiquity and associated Christian developments. While the living venerated their ancestors through proper burial and care for the dead, they also gained benefit in terms of social status derived from those practices. It was within the tomb that the dead become ancestors. The newly dead were placed on shelves and after decay, their bones were moved under the shelf or into a pit in the middle of the tomb. In that sense, they are 'gathered to their fathers' whose bones are also there. This is a classic expression of what anthropologists call double-burial, following Robert Hertz who depicted rites for the 'wet' corpse until it decays, then rites with the dry bones in ascribing a new ancestral identity (Hertz, [1905–6] 1960). In terms of worldviews, Suriano shifts attention away from some traditional Greek ideas of Plato, including those developed within Christian ideas of salvation, that assume soul to be immortal. The ancient Hebrew notion of soul, he says, is not immortal, but was more part and parcel of ongoing family-clan life aligned with tomb ritual, and passes away as kin ties move on. Still, both Judaism as a relatively self-contained cultural group and the Christian sect that emerged from it and expanded into a worldwide church host genealogical lists in their sacred texts, as in the Gospel of Matthew's first chapter with its 'account of the genealogy of Jesus the Messiah, the Son of David, the Son of Abraham' (Matthew 1:1–17).

Mormonism

Of all groups emerging within Christianity's broad flow, the Church of Jesus Christ of Latter-day Saints, established in 1830, possesses the strongest and most distinctive ancestral dimension. This mirrors aspects of the ancient tribes of Israel through ritual activities in which LDS individuals may receive a blessing from specially designated Patriarchs of the Church who are believed to deliver a special divine message about their personal life. Through the influence of the Holy Spirit Patriarchs tell people the tribe of Israel to which they belong. Besides this personalised rite, Mormons conduct extensive genealogical research that identifies ancestors and follows this up with 'temple work', including vicarious baptism and other initiatory rites for these identified dead. This extensive bureaucratic and ritual activity enhances links between the living and their dead, fostering their salvation in the eternal world, all within an ancestral worldview. This is substantiated in a way that echoes ancient Israel through the Church's two major forms of the Melchizedek and Aaronic Priesthoods whose work frames the role of the family, local church, and regional temple work, all contributing to its perspective on destiny. This strong family context of salvation is captured in the idiom of 'the soteriological lineage' (Davies, 2000:146–52). The complexity of the LDS Church is such that no single worldview embraces the totality of its outlook, so while the ancestral worldview is unmistakably significant, another of its properties will require further comment under the Prophetic worldview in a later chapter.

Confucianism

Highly influential in China as also in South Korea, Confucianism is also deeply 'social', according deep significance to relationships between parent and child, teacher and pupil, the living and the dead, all framed by its own ethical system of duty and obligation. Here the idea of 'respect' often appears as 'piety', with proper relationships contributing to the good order of society. While the question of the 'existence' of gods is largely irrelevant, the use of domestic shrines is widespread as are periodic family-focused rites of respect to the ancestors. The complexity of worldviews is highlighted in South Korea, for example, where Confucian ideas of respectful relationships and the aesthetic cultivation of texts emerged among older members of Christian congregations and the practice of copying out several versions of the Bible and presenting them to key family members and to Christian congregations. Here 'Christian' and 'Confucian' cultural practices feed off each other in contexts where Christian Churches slowly came to accept that local 'ancestor worship' was not a form of idolatry (Park, 2010).

Conclusion

These few cases, spread across time and place, represent many others where the dead continue to carry significance for the living, demonstrating how 'ordinary' kinship phenomena are sometimes intensified as formal institutions and ritual-symbolic processes.

9 Karmic worldview

Introduction

Just as ancestral worldviews mark an intensification of family dynamics, karmic worldviews intensify forms of social reciprocity. Daily life is grounded in multiple interrelationships of dutiful obligation with some key aspects transformed into universal processes involving rewards and punishments affecting the identity and destiny of people in afterlives of pain or pleasure. Notions of heaven and hell in Christianity, of Garden and a Fire in Islam, and of positive and negative reincarnations in some Indian traditions, all display the human expectation of give and take played out on a more elaborate and consequential stage.

So, although entitling this the karmic worldview because of its easy identification within Indian-derived traditions, its essential concern with moral action and reaction is evident in practically all worldview schemes. In those typified as 'religions', this is frequently associated with ideas of salvation allowing people to transcend the constraints and negativity of existence, but in others, the model of moral cause and effect is also evident. Still, this chapter will largely focus on Hindu and Buddhist themes, albeit with some references to Christianity and Islam to emphasise the ubiquity of reciprocal dynamics underlying processes of human identity and destiny. Although the Christian and Islamic notions of rewards and punishments associated with the afterlife are well-known they need complementing with the non-reward-based phenomena of divine grace that often appear in more mystical aspects of these traditions. Not only did notions of the immediacy of grace drive the Protestant Reformation in Christianity, but something similar is evident in Islam's Sufi mysticism, the Pure Land form of Japanese Buddhism, and bhakti forms of devotional Hinduism and Sikhism where dynamics of love and bonds of affection replace earned rewards.

DOI: 10.4324/9781003242437-12

The Indian matrix

Several traditions emerging from the Indian sub-continent, including Hindu, Buddhist, Jain and Sikh groups, are either rooted in or arose in opposition to the distinctive caste form of social organisation that structures society in a hierarchy of social groups related to a person's destiny. The logic of castes is the logic of reciprocity extended to identity and of different paths of access to a desired destiny. Although some of these are deeply theistic and others practically non-theistic, all approach the 'problem' of existence through the idea that appearance and reality are two different things, while differing in how to overcome the difficulty it presents.

The paths (marga)

For purposes of simplicity and clarity three basic pathways traverse the besetting problems of existence, pursuing philosophical, ethical, and devotion goals. First, often described as the way of knowledge or *jnanamarga* includes the issue of appearance-reality, contrasting what the world appears to be like with it really is. The second deals with *karma* (*karmamarga*) and gives some rationale for caste identity in everyday life in terms of previous existences and anticipation of future states. Third comes the realm of devotional love (*bhaktimarga*) of the bhakti traditions, where devotee and guru figure create a distinctive relationship, and this will reappear in the Mystical Worldview chapter. These rather abstract categories can run together in daily life, especially if approached in terms of identity and its fulfilment through insight, freedom, and release (*moksha*) from the life we now lead under the forces of karma.

In the age-old combination of *karma* and *caste*, the ethical worlds of action align with previous theoretical work on meaning-making, moral-rules, and merit. To follow social rules results in good karma, to disregard earns bad karma. Caste is a way of distinguishing between people on the grounds of their birth and the higher or lower level status of their birth-right groups. Caste or *varna* affects status in society and is traditionally referred to occupation; moreover, caste status is determined by one's karma in a previous life. The system depends upon the idea of transmigration or reincarnation, a scheme called samsara. In each existence, a person gains the outcome of their good or bad karma in a previous existence. This is a clear ethical system in which actions affect destiny. Some of the scriptures reinforce this view, as when the Bhagavad Gita asserts that it is better to do our own duty badly than someone else's duty well. Karma is gained in many ways, including making pilgrimages to holy places, itself a major form of embodied action. Some ethical reformers in India such as Mahatma Gandhi (1869–1948) came to object to this scheme when it meant that the lowest groups, described as outcaste groups, were badly treated by everyone else. In the main tradition, the only way out of this scheme was through many lives and application to caste duty in each of them, but modern issues of political reform could also be mobilised to attempt more 'this-worldly' settlement.

Caste and karma embrace the issue of embodiment through skin colour, occupation, food rules, and marriage options. By reflecting the moral state of a previous life, karma drives merit. Karma and merit are practically synonymous. And, just as a person's embodied form is what it is because of previous merit, so future embodiments will be determined by one's present life, until such time as I may be free from reincarnation and gain release or moksha. There is no clearer expression of the relationship between moral obedience to rules and their salvation outcome than in this case of caste rule, good karma and merit-acquisition, and destiny.

This caste scheme or *varnashramadharma* links caste (*varna*) with ideas of life stages (*ashrama*) through which – ideally – people pass as student, householder, semi-recluse and final recluse preparing for death, as well as with the *dharma* path of teaching. The broad caste division identifies Brahmins (priests), Kshatriyas (warriors), Vaishyas (merchants) and Sudras (outcaste), the first three being 'twice-born', and invested with a sacred thread over the shoulder at initiation rites of passage. Caste involves power differences and differences of social privilege with the issue of ritual purity being highly significant since higher caste persons can be rendered ritually impure by the wrong sort of contact with lower castes. Since most groups – often sub-castes jostling within their broad caste band – are ever trying to increase their status in relation to others, much attention is paid to who has dealings with whom. The prime values lying behind the caste system concern increased positive *karma* and the working towards ultimate release from reincarnation. Accordingly, ideas of ritual purity relate to hierarchy of status, especially the Brahmins whose status is most advanced in this scheme of things even though they may not possess the most material power or wealth. While the 'problem' of existence is overcome through many transmigrations and the making of merit it is rooted in daily acts. Still, even in this rule-based process, there are opportunities for early escape, whether by dying and being cremated in Banaras – a place of deep ritual purity, or through *bhakti* or devotional piety towards divinity. For many, however, transmigration remains the theoretical norm.

Buddhism

As for those following the Buddha, the path to enlightened knowing remains long. Millions pursue forms of observance as laity while some may become monks for short or lifelong periods and have special opportunity to make merit and share it with the laity. They, too, may make merit, not least in giving food to monks and gifts to monasteries. Amidst these reciprocal bonds, some traditions speak more personally of a compassionate Buddhist saviour figure while others dwell on more philosophical issues. To explore Buddhism is to acknowledge these issues of merit, divine assistance, and philosophical reflection, showing the complex worldviews framing Buddha pathways while also pointing to a worldview 'discovered'.

Buddhism as a discovery

What we call Buddhism would have emerged sooner or later whether or not Gautama, the fifth century north Indian had ever existed, or so Paul Williams with Anthony Tribe have argued (2000). Someone would have discovered the principles underlying the cosmos as now enshrined in the Dharma, the teaching that explains what came to be called the well-known four noble truths asserting that (a) suffering is basic to life – the outcome of *karma*; (b) desire – *tanha* – is the craving-lust that causes suffering; (c) suffering can cease, for there is a solution in the (d) Eightfold Path of correct knowledge, attitude, speech, action, living, effort, mindfulness, and composure.

Williams and Tribe identify Dharma as 'probably the single most important concept for understanding Indian religion' (2000:15). It expresses the cosmic law of suffering grounded in desire, its ending on the cessation of desire, or of craving (Sanskrit, *trsna* or thirst) – not only for material things but for existence and non-existence, and how to live to achieve that cessation (2000:440). The cessation is also an awakening of the mind where the naming of emotional states is brought within a philosophical frame that is also a broad notion of salvation. More technically we find a 'soteriology that sees the goal in terms of mental transformation ... it is in a sense a gnostic soteriology', something that everyone must discover for himself (2000:17). It is not achievable by austerity or by ritual but by 'knowing'. Urubshurow identifies dharma as 'the transcendent principle of the universe that upholds all existence', and the Buddha's teachings as 'Buddha-dharma', in that they were his discovery (2008:194). The Buddha-dharma serves as its own worldview, a high-range account of life, while a whole set of intersecting ideas or theories about the human condition furnishes a mid-range account of its implementation rooted in the deep desire or thirst (*tanha*) that binds folk to this world through many reincarnating existences or *samsara*. Peter Harvey speaks of this *samsara* as a kind of 'wandering on' (1994:12). Desire causes suffering and binds people with life's bitterness (*dukkha*), then actions (*karma*), especially bad actions, add a negative merit to our overall condition and set us all the more firmly within the *samsara* cycle of existence. For Harvey, *karma* is 'goodness-power' (1994:13), and the solution to the problem of existence coming in its cessation or cooling (*nibbana* in Buddhism's Pali language, *nirvana* in Hinduism's Sanskrit), made possible through renunciation of desire and the negative way of life that fosters and enacts desire.

These ideas stand on their own as teachings open for all to follow, but historically, they have been focused on and understood through the individual called Gautama, who is *nibbuta* – or has 'cooled'.

The Buddha's approach is often described as a middle way, practised primarily by monks who live in community (the *sangha*), where their capacity to observe the precepts and make merit is easier than that of the laity whose engagement with the teachings and the ideal way of life is less possible because of their duties in making a living (Tambiah, 1968).

Gautama

As with most worldviews, their ideal, abstract, and formal nature benefits enormously from a narrative base, especially if exemplified through the life of distinctive individuals. Whether this is more factually historical, hagiographic, or even mythical in form is often of secondary significance because people seem to prefer to deal with 'ideas' as they take shape in someone's life. It is easier to identity with someone else's life and its emotional and relationships turns than with purely abstract formulations of existence.

The life of Gautama, someone seeking meaning in his own day, era, and personal circumstances, was one such. With Gautama, as with Guru Nanak, Jesus, Mohammad, Joseph Smith, and many other religious founders and leaders, the ongoing traditions that increasingly framed their ideas develop narratives allowing devotees of all ranges of understanding and interest to gain some grasp of their tradition. More than this, such narratives allow people to relate their own life-story as a kind of mini-narrative to the grand-narrative of the broad tradition that fosters their identity and promises some kind of worthwhile destiny. In this way, an emergent worldview often takes shape in a personalised form, and in this case of Gautama, we encounter a relatively well-off youth, comfortable and married at 16, who becomes troubled by life's problems.

The traditional story tells of his rather protected life, even a royal lifestyle in later traditions, until he finds himself confronted by a sick, an old, and a dead man. He realised that old-age, sickness, and death would, one day, reach him, and wondered how he might escape them, or at least escape the trouble they caused his mind. Then he sees a religious ascetic and is attracted to that lifestyle. Thus emerges the realisation that life is problematic, distressing, and aligned with a problematic flaw in existence, in this case identified as suffering and death. In trying to find an answer, he first employed asceticism, leaving his wife and son behind and engaging in fasting. But he found that this did not bring him the desired answer. He then adopted a less austere stance, often called the middle way, one involving meditation. This was an intensive period and included his being tempted by a kind of personification of evil (*Mara*) but he won through to new understanding and to 'seeing how things are including the idea of "not-self" (*anatman*) and of impermanence (*anicca*)', two key concepts responding to that knowledge. For most western-influenced people, the 'not-self' idea is particularly hard to understand. Indeed, the very term 'understand' is itself problematic when taken as some kind of logical process of rationalising, separate from emotional intuitions arising within the meditative processes of the Dharma-path. 'There is absolutely no suggestion that the Buddha thought there is some additional factor called the Self ... [A]n unchanging element, the real "me", a Self, is simply non-existent' (Williams and Tribe, 2000:61–2).

For Gautama, however, narratives speak of a kind of waking up from the sleepy state of ordinary existence. Terms such as 'awareness' or 'mindfulness' are helpful here and hint at the creative application of someone to the world, emphasising the place of a kind of philosophical analysis of existence, emotions, and motivations in relation to our actual way of life. As Urubshurow starkly expressed it, 'he woke up to see reality as it is'. (2008:194). The Buddha becomes an exemplar, showing the possibility of insight, awakening, and of ensuing compassion, and then dying as an old man of about eighty years of age sometime around 400 BCE. His was a world of numerous groups of people with religious teachings about life, including what we now call parts of Hinduism. Williams describes him as a 'dropout', and uses stories about his life as a way into understanding the discovery of the Dharma, always recalling that Gautama stories are hagiographies, accounts written by followers with strong theological motives.

Narratives, institutions, and lifestyles

Narratives express worldviews and have a power to draw people into their way of seeing things, especially when social patterns emerge that reflect and reinforce their ideals. The emergence of the Sangha as a community of monks dedicated to core values but intimately connected to a lay public reflects the idea that a lay way of life is not, in a sense, the ideal way because it inevitably involves negative merit, for the householder needs to be caught up in worldly care, must engage in sex to reproduce the species and engage in work that could be harmful to living things. This special reciprocal relationship between monks and laity involves teaching and learning but also in the laity giving and the monks receiving food and material support but also in the monks giving and laity receiving merit. In what is a form of division of labour, the monks live according to the rules and make merit that can be shared with the laity, while the laity's pragmatic life-work allows them to give material gifts to the monks. Merit, when transferred to the laity, can aid them in their next incarnation and in other ways too. This spatial and social organisation of temple, monks, and Sangha on the one hand, and village and laity on the other speaks to the ideals and doctrines advocated by the Buddhist perspective. From this relatively simple scheme of monks and laity, Noble Truths and paths, complex schools have emerged facilitated by the relative abandonment of caste ideas alongside the potential of lay-forms of practice as is now evident in many contemporary 'modern' societies in Europe, the USA, and beyond.

History also shows how an ideology such as Buddhism can become an extensive worldview with wide political consequences as well as more personalised religiosity, as with the remarkable King Ashoka (304–232 BC). He developed a kingdom across most of the Indian sub-continent (269–232 BC) having renounced his previous bloodthirsty conquests, he became pacifist, adopted Buddhism, and helped make it possible for Buddhism to develop across the Far East, even though it dramatically declined in India after his day. In some ways, Ashoka's adoption of Buddhism, following a battle and his response to bloodshed, is not unlike the western Emperor Constantine's fostering of Christianity from around 313 AD, often associated with his belief in the appearance of a cross in the skies before the battle of the Milvan Bridge AD 312.

Theoretical aspects of a worldview context

Worldviews are, then, expressed through many dimensions of social and cultural life, some dealing with abstract ways of thinking and others with narrative forms embracing basic aspects of material culture, practical behaviour, and polity. A variety of theoretical ideas that can be brought to an analysis of these both here and in other chapters include those of embodiment, symbolism, and merit-making.

Embodiment and symbolism

Ideas associated with Gautama, the Buddha, are aligned with material representations in statues, artistic representations of many forms, as well as in stories about his life and teaching. These provide a focus for laity as well as monks. Seated, lying or standing, Buddha is depicted in meditation, showing what it means to have the insight of *nibbana*. Sometimes he appears almost as a skeleton when in his ascetic attempts at enlightenment, others depict non-austerity. The Sangha, in its turn, furnishes an expression of the Buddha's Noble Path. In the form of a living community whose way of life is daily visible to the laity, it touches families as sons or daughters become monks or nuns either for a lifetime or for short periods of time. They too may become an embodiment of the truths, for Buddhist ideals are open to all. In Tibetan Buddhist tradition, especially in the Dalai Lama, and other key figures, those who could gain release from samsara elect to be reincarnated out of compassion for those not so advanced. These are symbols; they participate in what they represent, the ideals are partially made manifest.

Merit, merit-making, and receiving

Buddhism has developed a worldview involving a complex interplay between monks and the laity. Both can make merit and share it, but monks make more, because lay-life makes observance of all desired precepts impossible. In terms of a great deal of popular Buddhism in the countries where it became naturalised, rites for the making of merit became common, given 'how a lay public rooted in this world can adhere to a religion committed to the renunciation of the world', and 'the remoteness of Nirvana ideal for the layman' (Tambiah, 1968:41–2). Lay folk give regular gifts of food and have periodic dealings with the local temple and give gifts to it, while the monks provide merit in return. Gaining good karma involves a sense that it will help one's death and the immediate existence after death while also giving a kind of contentment during life. The sense of an account between good and bad karma involves ideas of a good-existence after death drawing on the good-karma capital before having to return to earth. This *samsara* scheme is, itself, far from the ideal of Buddhism which is to escape the *samsara* cycle. That takes an act of will and the choice of taking up the Noble Eightfold path of renunciation in moving towards enlightenment.

Buddhism offers a classic context for discussing merit, merit-making, and the use of merit as analysed, for example, by both Tambiah (1968) and Obeyesekere (1968). Tambiah spells out much that has been said above as he depicts real-life contexts.

> Life lived in accord with Dharma would not attract the effect of karma and thus not lead to rebirth, but that is a difficult way of existence. Yet the belief emerged that it was possible to make some merit and improve one's condition either in this life or in the next incarnation. To become a monk would help whether for a temporary period or for life. Such merit might also be used to benefit others. In terms of a great deal of popular Buddhism in the countries where it became naturalised,

rites for the making of merit became common given 'the remoteness of Nirvana ideal for the layman'.

(Tambiah, 1968:42)

In thinking like this, we are drawing on the idea of merit as a kind of salvation commodity and framing it as a kind of 'goodness-power' that can be shared (Harvey, 2002:15). In many practical Buddhist contexts, the sense of a commodity that can be shared takes visible and tangible forms. One example experienced by the present author took place in a Buddhist temple in the North-East of England in 2019. It had been adapted from what had been a Christian church and is now a thriving Buddhist centre. At the annual day when the laity offer gifts to the temple and monks and gain merit in the process, a new stained glass window depicting the life of the Buddha was dedicated. At one crucial point of the ceremony, focused on the act of dedication of the window, but set within the overall ceremonial of the day, a senior monk led a procession of visiting dignitaries and donors up to the window, set in a first-floor gallery, and engaged in dedicatory chanting of texts. That ritual specialist, at a set point in the proceedings, took hold of a ribbon that led to an entire network of ribbons spread throughout the building with each person present holding on to one piece of ribbon coming to them from its network. The tone of the event was solemn, and explanations of this practice turned on the people present, notably the large number of lay people present sharing in the merit made through the gift and dedication of the window.

Philosophical reflections

That highly practical context of merit-making and merit-receiving was set in a day of devotional chanting and teaching, with many other gifts being offered to the monks, both inside the temple, and in an outside ceremony when the monks passed in procession along a very long row of lay-devotees, each giving material gifts to the passing monks. Many smaller examples of material gifts given to monks and immaterial merit being received from them occur daily in countries with Buddhist cultural traditions. Within those cultural traditions, however, some monks and laity pay considerable attention to more abstract reflections on the Dharma, including such ideas as non-permanent selfhood. This interplay of pragmatic ritual behaviour and abstract philosophical deliberation occurs in practically all worldview traditions.

From a social scientific perspective, this notion of the non-enduring self is particularly interesting in terms of meaning-making, identity, and destiny, especially given that sociologists of religion emphasise language and community in forging a sense of reality. What then, if that sense of reality is believed to be false and deceptive? How should language then be viewed? With Buddhism as with all traditions of life-analysis and life-direction, both philosophy and abstraction on the one hand and practical behavioural on the other often complement each other. Moreover, some may use one aspect of a tradition for one life-domain and another for other demands. In contemporary Japan, for example, a person might well be married through Christian and buried by Buddhist rites. This seems strange to a traditional Christian culture where exclusivity predominates but not in other contexts of eclectic traditions.

Some issues affecting worldviews are shared across cultural traditions, as between Buddhist and western philosophical concerns with language and identity. For example, Tetsuaki Kotoh (1992) asked whether language makes human being or human being makes language. He favours the latter within a discussion of the total nothingness of life and of the 'double-concealment' by which, in 'pleasant somnolence', people live oblivious of that nothingness and in an escape from ourselves (1992:33). His concern, emerging from Zen Buddhism, is with the very nature of human existence as explored in western philosophy by the philosophers Heidegger (1889–1976) and Gadamer (1900–2002). In certain important respects, this philosophical tradition mirrors the sociological and anthropological concerns with language as factors that help construct personal identity and social worlds. Kotoh argues that self-transformation is possible through a breakdown of the structure of language that allows silence to emerge. For him, such silence can come to be the basis of and for a sense of self that seeks neither to flee from itself nor from the senselessness of existence. Here he praises Heidegger's acknowledgement of the intimate link between 'language and the ground of self (silence)' (1992:42). Kotoh develops this relationship between language and silence in terms of a person possessing a right attitude, a sense of self and of world that acknowledges meaninglessness without being dismayed. This brings the notion of silence into play in a dramatic and telling fashion, not as a negative and oppressive silence but as a creative fount. Kotoh wishes to emphasise this place of silence at the heart of Being in Heidegger's thought, viewing silence as a positive source of language and of the linguistic persons humans come to be.

This case raises the question of how different religions use language as part of the fabric of their worldviews. What value do they give it, and how do they use it in relation to their perceived ultimate goals? The Hindu meditative use of the *mantra* – a verse from a sacred text – is developed as a desired daily mental state, not least in the Sikh ideal of dwelling upon the name of God (*Nam simran*). The use of scriptures in Judaism, Christianity, and Islam can all be explored in this connection. Scriptures are used as a medium of revelation and of devotion: they are chanted and studied and in and through prayers, they become embodied as part of a devotee's self-understanding. In newly evolving Pagan rites in modern societies, language also assumes declarative and formulaic patterns that symbolise the power of the natural world of energies desired by devotees.

Conclusion

This chapter has shown how a dominant concept, in this case karma and the idea of merit, can emerge from the ordinary dynamics of human life and be intensified into a cosmic principle while remaining open for analysis through the social science of reciprocity theory. This complex of karma, merit, and the transmigrating of a life-force has fostered patterns of behaviour and thought involving considerable complexity manifest in the architecture of temples, the social organisation of the Sangha community of monks, and their relationships with the laity directed towards ideas of destiny. This complexity has accompanied the rise and fall of empires as well as life practices exported across the world. Moreover, some Indian-derived schools of thought did this in alliance with ideas of deities and others without that commitment. The knowledge inspiring these traditions also came by different routes, sometimes as innovative insights and sometimes as revelations, and it is to one dynamic cluster of sources that the next chapter directs attention, that of prophets and sects.

10 Prophetic-sectarian

Introduction

Worldviews change when rejected, supplanted, or slowly transformed or when their existing orthodoxies are reformed or renewed. This chapter introduces some relatively well-known aspects of such change in terms of prophets, their charismatic attributes, and the sects they sometimes instigate. It also presents one innovative sketch of early Christian sectarianism that revisits the theme of reciprocity and identity.

Prophets, Charisma, and Max Weber (1864–1920)

A prophet speaks potentially powerful words and is described by Weber as 'a purely individual bearer of charisma, who by virtue of his mission proclaims a religious doctrine or divine commandment' (1922:46). Making no distinction between a 'renewer of religion' and a 'founder of a religion', Weber highlights their 'personal call' as a vital element. Although in Christian heritage societies, people often speak of priests as having a 'vocation' or calling to church ministry, Weber takes the prophetic call to another level of significance, for priests have authority granted to them by pre-existing religious institutions while prophets – at the outset – often stand alone. Theoretically speaking, the idea of prophets and the charismatic relationships they have with their followers depicts two modes of human meaning-making. One reflects their formal message of interest to theology, philosophy, and the sociology of religion, and the other reflects the ritual-symbolic aspects of behaviour often studied by anthropologists. In practice, prophets often help people make sense of the world, especially during times of change when ritual-symbolic behaviour helps to work out the message in practical ways that nurture life's emotions. Over time, however, that emotional impact may become redirected to more formal and bureaucratic institutions in what Weber described as the 'routinization of charisma' (Kasler, 1988:164).

DOI: 10.4324/9781003242437-13

Weber categorised two main prophetic types: ethical and exemplary. Ethical prophets appear in many of the Hebrew Bible's leading figures, as well as in Islam's Muhammad, and Persia's Zoroaster. These announce divine messages and call people to responsive obedience, whereas exemplary prophets, not least the Buddha, show people how to live. Still, Weber highlights the place of coherent meaning in life for both types of a prophet and stresses the place of conduct as the medium through which salvation may come. In all of this, the importance of meaning-making is given high profile as is the idea of people's orientation to the world, a concept that is practically synonymous with 'worldview' in Weber's work.

Wilson: types, 'evil', and salvation

One instructive way of approaching worldviews follows on from Weber's orientation to the word and is found in various sociological classifications of religious organisations such as churches, denominations, and sects. Here we focus on one well-known example originating with Bryan R. Wilson (1926–2004). Much influenced by Weber, Ernst Troeltsch, and others, he constructed a classification or typology of sects driven through an analysis of how groups depicted flaws in existence and how they set about overcoming them (Wilson, 1970). The following quotation shows a stress on 'evil' and 'demand for reassurance' that, in many respects, could be taken as one valuable indicative definition of religion at large.

> Men seek salvation from evil conceived in many forms – from anxiety; illness; inferiority feelings; grief; fear of death; concern for the social order. What they seek may be healing; the elimination of evil agents; a sense of access to power; the promise of life hereafter, or reincarnation, or resurrection from the grave, or attention from posterity; the transformation of the social order (including the restoration of a real or imagined past order). The common core of all these specific forms of salvation is the demand for reassurance.
>
> (1973:492)

This 'demand for reassurance' echoes the human drive for meaning at both emotional and intellectual levels. It is typical of how worldviews in general sustain human identity but is especially applicable in sects as a social microcosm.

Wilson typified sects at large as possessing voluntary and exclusive membership principles, a strong internalising of the group's principles, and tests of merit running alongside the possibility of expulsion for unworthy members. Advantages of membership include elite status and privileged access to truth assured by the authority of a charismatic leadership, whether in religion or politics (Aberbach, 1996). Some sects manifest high and some low levels of these features, a variation depending on the stage of development of the movement. Crucially, Wilson could, for example, have chosen styles of leadership, attitude to money, or family organisation as the basis for his classification, but his stress fell upon 'evil'. This reflects Weber's influence on Wilson in terms of people's 'orientation to the world', 'need for salvation', 'thirst for life', and 'quest for salvation' (Weber, [1922] 1964:139,146,149). One of Wilson's key formulations appeared as a sevenfold typology described here by their type of sect, the form evil takes, and the prime response to evil.

(a) Conversionists root evil in the human heart, with salvation requiring converted hearts, as in Evangelical Christianity. (b) Reformists see social structures as evil and awaiting rational-political change, as in modern Quakers. (c) Revolutionists also see societies as evil but await God's intervention for change, as with today's Jehovah's Witnesses. (d) Introversionists see human relationships in need of transformation and, like the Mennonites or Hutterites, seek to establish their own communities. (e) Utopian groups also see social relationships in need of change and pursue group salvation as with the Oneida Community. (f) Manipulationist sects pinpoint distinctive phenomena as evil and deploy manipulative techniques to overcome them, as with Christian Science and Scientology with their theories of mind over matter. (g) Thaumaturgical or wonder-working sects also pinpoint symbols of evil and exert control over them, as many Charismatic Christian groups and, very much smaller in number – Snake Handling groups in the USA (Wilson, 1970).

Wilson, Evans-Pritchard, and 'Evil'

As a distinctively speculative note, it might be that Weber's expressly sociological influence on Wilson should be complemented by the social anthropology of E. E. Evans-Pritchard, especially in helping to shape Wilson's view of 'evil'. Put briefly, Evans-Pritchard (1902–1973) was one of the most famous twentieth-century anthropologists, whose ethnographic studies included work on how the Azande of North Central Africa and the Sudan conceived of misfortune and disaster in terms of witchcraft and sought to overcome them through oracles and practical magical rites (1937). Wilson was very familiar with Evans-Pritchard's work and was, for example, thanked by Evans-Pritchard for reading a draft of his later *Theories of Primitive Religion* (1967). This was a natural consequence of their familiarity as contemporary Fellows of All Souls College Oxford. This brief example of the interplay of theoretical sociology and a detailed ethnographic study in anthropology is indicative of the creative interplay of ideas in the mind of a considerable scholar of religion.

Charismatic persons

To those disciplinary influences, the following now adds a psychological–psychiatric perspective to the theme of charisma, especially as it also takes effect in political contexts. The key link is forged between Wilson on 'reassurance' and the psychiatrist Anthony Storr on "certainty" as being highly seductive', 'offered by all successful leaders', and 'an important part of charisma' (Storr, 1997:217). This case could equally well be placed as an example in the 'Ideological worldview' but it also fits here. It is presented in narrative terms much as Storr recounts experiences with both Oswald Mosely and Winston Churchill – two similar yet quite different political figures of Britain's mid-twentieth century.

Storr describes a dinner party that included Sir Oswald Mosely, 'whose political stance and particularly his antisemitism were anathema to me ... the first impression he made was of a courteous, old fashioned aristocrat with beautiful manners. Mosely had immense charm'. When the conversation shifted to the political problems of Northern Ireland, he propounded solutions that the government ought to adopt. Storr continued,

> Although Mosely had long been discredited, I began to understand why, in his early days, he had been hailed as a future Prime Minister. He was so convincing that one began to feel that he might be right ... perhaps Mosely really *knew* ... Against my own better judgement, I became fleetingly impressed by a man whose former policies I hated, simply because he appeared so sure that he was right.
>
> (1997:219)

This exemplifies the force of certainty driving the potential of charismatic appeal to a listener, even a psychiatrist as astute as Storr. Mosley's fascism had, in fact, come to nothing despite much political conflict and even social riot. By contrast, Churchill's complex political path climaxed in his political leadership during the Second World War. Here Storr's analysis links Churchill's internal fantasy with the needs of people. In a case with potential wide interest to all religious and political prophets and revolutionaries, he portrays the correlation between the inner fantasy of prophet-charismatic types and the needs of large-scale groups. Private fantasy is one thing, a shared fantasy taken up by others is quite another, and brings with it a reinforcement of the personal 'vision' and, we might say, a 'reassurance' of its nature.

His description draws from accounts of Churchill's life, including that by Lord Moran, Churchill's most distinguished physician. This involved Churchill's 'inner world of make-belief' – what Storr takes as fantasy, and included Churchill's sense that, when he was made Prime Minister, aged sixty-five, with the War raging and Britain in severe peril, he tells his doctor – 'This cannot be accident, it must be design. I was kept for this job' (Storr, 1997:217).

Storr goes on to speak of Churchill as 'idolized as the saviour of the country': his 'well-nigh miraculous achievement during the dire summer months of 1940 was to convert the nation to a mystical faith in its own providential destiny'. This, Storr, thinks, 'throws light on that mysterious quality of charisma which is so characteristic of gurus'. Storr emphasises the inner fantasy world of a person, and of how Churchill was able 'to impose it upon almost the whole British population at a time when a hero was desperately needed'. Storr invokes the notion of psychological narcissism in this; 'Churchill was intensely narcissistic'. 'In 1940, Churchill became the hero that he had always dreamed of being. It was his finest hour … his inspirational quality owed its dynamic force to the romantic world of fantasy in which he had his true being' (1997:218).

The issue of a personal call is interesting in terms of Storr's stress on a person's inner-life and fantasy worlds, and parallels Weber on 'calling' or 'vocation'. In other words, a prophet's sense of call offers a self-frame as someone special. If and when that personal sense is matched by the attractive power of the person to whom others turn and who they follow, then we are amidst a new religious grouping and potentially of a new worldview. This shows how important certain individuals can be if their inner sense of meaning-making gains public expression when social conditions are ripe for criticism and change. It also reinforces Wilson when he speaks of charisma as a relationship and not just 'a quality of a person', for it 'contains the acceptability of a leader by a following; the endorsement of his personality, and the social endowment of power'. Indeed, he coins the phrase 'charismatic demand' to cover contexts where 'men mobilize as a following and look for a leader' (1973:499).

Charisma, group, and merit

This final account brings together the themes of charismatic leaders and community, reciprocity and merit, identity, and the power of narrative, all within the emergent Christian sect portrayed in the biblical Acts of the Apostles. While it tells of charismatic forces of attraction in specified leaders such as Peter and Paul and those surrounding them, it is the theological phenomenon of the Holy Spirit as the generative core of this community that underlies the stories that are told. Drawing from previous discussions of reciprocity theory in both its threefold and fourth obligation, much analytical sense can be made of these dramatic episodes (Davies, 2004:259–80). Essentially, the Holy Spirit – as the generative source of this community, and which serves as a powerful 'replacement' of the resurrected Jesus – is presented as the group's core cultural value, with participation in that resource and group being expressed through a person's attitude to money and the worth of things. Authenticity of membership depends upon sincerity in using goods, so too with inauthenticity, duplicity, and betrayal.

Acts of the Apostles authenticity of membership

In the narrative flow of The Acts of the Apostles, Judas betrays his master for money (1:18), while true believers sell their possessions and give to the common purse (2:44–45. 4:34–35). Peter possesses nothing except his owning the name of Jesus (3:6). Converted magicians burn their books whose value is noted (19:19). Paul cannot be bribed (24:26), and pays his own way (28:30) thus proving his Christian integrity. By sharp contrast, though echoing Judas, Ananias and Saphira pretend to sell and give to the community but cheat and thereby betray the Spirit: their insincerity, like that of Judas, leads to their death (5:1–10). Another convert, Simon the magician, seeks to purchase the charismatic power of the Apostles and finds himself in a perilous situation (8:20). In analytical terms, this suggests that both Jesus and the Holy Spirit are inalienable gifts, beyond price. To be genuinely Christian is to know that 'inalienability', often as interpreted as a form of 'grace', related to divine goodwill and love, and not as something that can be earned or purchased. For the Master or Rabbi to be 'sold' or betrayed for the proverbial 'pieces of silver' (1:18) is as perverse as any relationship can get: Paul on the other hand is depicted as reliability incarnate. At the outset he is firmly opposed to Jesus and the Christian movement, but after his conversion he is firm in his new commitment and cannot be 'bought' by bribe or the like. Similarly the 'Spirit' or the power of the spirit cannot be bought as Simon the magician desired, his name also becoming fixed in the notion of Simony. In an intriguing sense, 'money' becomes the medium of expressing sincere participation in the community of the Spirit.

One key theological idea that emerges from this community dynamic is that faith, and salvation as a form of identity, emerge from participation in the community engendered by the Holy Spirit, and often described as the body of Christ. Many divisive arguments fill succeeding millennia as to how individuals access salvation, especially when the idea of merit is brought into the discussion. Merit as 'salvation stuff', already discussed in the Karmic Worldview, develops in complex grammars of theological discourse and Christian history, not least involving the Protestant Reformation.

In much Protestant thought, it became dangerous to talk of merit apart from Jesus Christ, especially in terms of other sorts of merit generated by the Catholic Church, Saints, and martyrs. The Protestant Reformation was utterly sensitive to this problem of merit-acquisition, occasioned by the nature of Catholic indulgences – documents that could be purchased from church agents whose authority would ensure a more favourable state in the afterlife for those for whom the indulgence was intended. This was feasible because of the 'treasury of merit' of the church. In theological terms, it was not that reformation theology had no place for merit or for merit-transfer, but it simply disagreed with its source and method of transfer. Reformation theology vested all merit in Christ and nowhere else. His was the perfectly obedient life. Salvation lay in receiving merit from Christ, a process framed by the utter grace of God. Merit-transfer from Christ to sinner was also allied with 'faith', itself a relational attitude to God and Christ: but the salvation that Christ's merit brought was not to come through priestly mediation of church agents but through faith framed by divine grace. These very issues transformed the world inasmuch as the Catholic–Protestant divide transformed Europe and was exported across the globe in distinctive patterns of worldviews, a point taken up and much debated in the light of Max Weber's theory of the Protestant Ethic (1976). It argued that the Protestant doctrine of God's inscrutable will that eternally divided believers into the saved and the damned made devotees uneasy because no one could know with certainty who was on each list. To compensate for this, believers devoted themselves to religious duties and when they flourished through sound capitalist principles, they took this as a sign that God blesses his people, and assumed that they must be amongst the saved.

Conclusion

This chapter has shown something of the variety of influence of people and groups upon the emergence of worldviews. The emotional dynamics of charisma centred on prophets and more distributed in sects may often fail with time, but some prosper (Dawson, 1998). The rise of a small sect of Judaism into worldwide churches creating entire worldviews is astonishing, so too with each of the world religious traditions, as their narrative accounts of lives invite new generations to merge their mini-autobiographies with the grand narrative of faith, identity, and destiny.

11 Mystical worldview

Introduction

To speak of a mystical worldview is unusual because mystical elements are often relegated to life's margins rather than to the organisational mainstream of a group, and because of the difficulty in defining 'mystery' and 'mystical'. Yet many charismatic and ritual-symbolic contexts integrate emotional with doctrinal factors in ways that form and foster devotees amidst mystical niches of their dominant perspectives. This needs emphasis, given that the emotion-rooted base of human life is often overlooked in studies of religion that focus on history, texts, doctrine, and philosophy.

Emotions and mysticism

To the previous chapter's spotlight on Wilson's 'demand for reassurance' in the life of sects, this chapter adds mysticism as one prime form of emotional reassurance that brings with it a cognitive satisfaction of 'knowing' the truthfulness or the reality of existence. Because human life is perilous, with people being often afraid of others, of dangerous circumstances, and often of death, worldviews often succeed by offering refuge from alarm. Buddhism offers refuge in its major rites, teachings, and figures. So too with Hare Krishna devotion, Sikh meditative practice and the sheer existence of the Guru grounded community, and not forgetting Islam's Sufi groups. Judaism has its own forms of mystical tradition as does Christianity. A dominant feature of these is some notion of love and attachment between devotee and the divine. Here again we find an ordinary aspect of life – the comfort of another person, say a mother or father – intensified in a religious frame. One classic criticism of this fear-refuge approach lies in Freud on religion as wish-fulfilment towards a heavenly father, given the ultimate failure of earthly parents and their mortality (1960). Today a more compelling approach comes from studies of kinds of human attachment (Granqvist, 2020).

DOI: 10.4324/9781003242437-14

Mysticism is one style of meaning-making, rooted in the impact of emotional awareness upon a person's grasp of the significance of life, even if of
a single or infrequent occurrence. Although mystics speak much of it, they
regularly describe their experience as ineffable – or being unable to capture
in words. While speaking much of the unspeakable may seem paradoxical,
its contradiction is unravelled once we see the mystic as narrating autobiographical events. In other words, it is the recognition of the force of a
significant affective–cognitive event amidst life's experiences that counts,
more than the ability to detail its content. Mystics are well-known across
time, as with Julian of Norwich (c. 1342–1416) or John of the Cross (1542–
1591). At the end of the nineteenth and early twentieth centuries, there was
something of a heightened interest in Mysticism as a kind of universal experience that could transcend different world religious traditions. The famous
Dean Inge (1860–1954) of St Paul's Cathedral was one contributor to this
phenomenon that paralleled an interest in the 'religions of the East' as with
Madame Blavatsky (1831–1881) the Russian occultist who founded the
Theosophical Society in the late nineteenth century. On another front, the
relative popularity of Spiritualism that straddled the nineteenth and twentieth centuries and remains an active though minority movement in today's
world might also be viewed as a form of mysticism. This moot point is
worthy of deeper analysis than can be pursued here.

James and Benson

Still, the twentieth century's contribution to the study of mysticism is extensive. It notably includes William James (1842–1910) whose *The Varieties
of Religious Experience* (1902) described and categorised different kinds
of religious experience, notably the 'once-born' type of religion of healthy-
mindedness, and the 'twice-born' religion of the sick soul – with its 'born-
again' characteristic later captured in Wilson's 'conversionist sect'. James
also depicts experiences of moments of transformation, including a sense of
oneness with the universe. From a more medical-psychological approach,
Herbert Benson studied forms of changed awareness, insightful moments,
and the sense of revelation. These all carry wide application. One key work
described 'the relaxation response' triggered by a meditative focus on sight
or sound that activates a biochemical-nervous response that is the opposite of the well-known flight or fight response (Benson and Klipper, 1975).
This very natural phenomenon can, easily, be adopted and given a distinctive 'mystical' or broader religious frame by groups such as Transcendental
Meditation that build it into their ritual-symbolic religious tradition. Today,
one of the major expressions of this approach is that of Mindfulness, which
has an enormous impact in a variety of contexts. Some see it as a fairly

direct appropriation, albeit with a removal of the 'religious' frame, of what, for example, Buddhist traditions have been practising for millennia. The key is that meditative practice – something that has to be practised and not simply talked about – makes its own impact upon a person's awareness in ways that become self-validating. Mark Williams (born 1952), an Oxford professor of psychology, has done much to encourage such 'mindfulness' practice. In many of these activities, a certain domestication or even democratisation of 'mysticism', or at least of mystery-like moments, takes place.

Albert Schweitzer (1875–1965)

Today, the profound significance of ecology and environmentalism also recharges the significance of mystical elements of a worldview with an emphasis not on some worldwide, inter-religious shared experience, nor on an individual person's enhancement of self-identity through meditation, but more as a recognised sense of the integration of all life-forms. Being 'at one' with nature has shifted from the luxury of enhanced selfhood to the necessity of people's pragmatic participation in the earth's living network as demonstrated in some previous chapters.

One of its profoundest philosophical–theological foundations lies in Albert Schweitzer's notion of 'reverence for nature'. This is described further but needs to be set alongside a kind of mysticism drawn from his explicitly theological–biblical studies captured in the idea of Christ-mysticism. To align these is to gain a fuller sense of Schweitzer, and an appreciation of the role of narrative in framing his personal perspective which did not always resonate with wider European worldviews, and which contradicted them in terms of peace and war. Yet his vision of faith and of nature, however personally rooted, found a considerable following in due course and still carries a resonance in today's world. This case serves as an important reminder, one echoed throughout this book, that the individual biography of influential people should never be forgotten when accounting for their influence upon worldviews. So, what of Schweitzer?

Schweitzer first qualified in theology and philosophy and when already well established as a European intellectual undertook medical training to become a medical missionary at Lambarené in the French Congo in 1913 and 1924. Many saw the location as the back of beyond and wondered why such a high-profile person should commit himself to such a low-profile place. But, as ever, such judgements lie in a person's own judgement, especially when the idea of a vocation or calling is at stake, as in his case. He had been a prisoner of war 1917–1918, and spent 1918–1924 preaching and giving organ recitals in Europe to gather funds for his African medical work. He was a considerable organist and wrote extensively on Johann Sebastian Bach. In

1955, he was awarded the Nobel Peace Prize. Here, in one of the greatest Christian thinkers and exemplars of the nineteenth-twentieth centuries, we encounter a distinctive individual with a personal mystical orientation expressed through a double-impact mysticism, one focused on Christ and another on 'Life' evident in the world at large. In this, he explicitly engages with ideas of *weltanshauung* or worldview as now explored for each domain.

Christ-mysticism

At the close of his 1901 study published in English as *The Mystery of the Kingdom of God: The Secret of Jesus' Messiahship and Passion*, Schweitzer speaks of 'The heroic' as receding from 'our modern "Weltanschauung", our Christianity, and our conception of the person of Jesus', arguing that 'our generation has modernised him, with the notion that it could comprehend his character and development psychologically'. He goes on,

> We must go back to the point where we can feel again the heroic Jesus. Before that mysterious Person, who, in the form of his time, knew that he was creating upon the foundation of his life and death a moral world which bears his name, we must be forced to lay our faces in the dust, without daring even to wish to understand his nature. Only then can the heroic in our Christianity and in our 'Weltanschauung' be again revived.
> ([1901] 1950:274–75)

Schweitzer took his strong perspective on mysticism into his study of *The Mysticism of Paul the Apostle* (1931) where he identifies Paul's doctrine and life-experience as that of a 'dying and rising with Christ, which was born out of Christianity itself, and becomes for every man who seeks new life in Christ a truth continually renewed, at once primitive and permanent', and also 'brings us into an inner controversy with our own existence, which extends itself into ever widening circles' ([1931] 1953:387). His *Quest for the Historical Jesus* (1906) also prompted much theological debate and closes with a mystical-like appreciation of Jesus who comes to today's faithful 'as one unknown', yet saying, 'Follow thou me'. To take up that call is to know conflict and suffering but, 'as an ineffable mystery, they shall learn in their own experience Who He is'.

Reverence for life mysticism

It is in the light of these explicitly theological and personal spiritual applications of 'mysticism' that Schweitzer's notion of 'Reverence for Life' can be presented as its own form of mysticism. Two pointers, one from a sermon and another from his autobiography, will map his mystical appreciation of 'life'.

The first pinpoints 'All knowledge' as ultimately, 'knowledge of life. All realization is amazement at this riddle of life – a reverence for life in its infinite and yet ever-fresh manifestation'. Schweitzer sees himself in everything; 'the tiny beetle that lies dead in your path – it was a living creature, struggling for existence like yourself, rejoicing in the sun like you, knowing fear and pain like you. And now it is no more than decaying matter – which is what you will be sooner or later, too'. This leads him to ask 'how are we to build a new humanity? Only by leading men toward a true inalienable ethic of our own ... the great commandment which is: Reverence for Life' ([1966] 1974:116–17).

The second is an even stronger stress on an emotional grasping of something. This theologian–philosopher–doctor was, by 1915 and aged forty, in a deep mental and existential confusion amidst the First Great War between great European Christian civilisations. He wondered how it had come to this, given that the nineteenth century had produced a sense of progress and life-affirmation. Ideas of worldview, civilisation, and ethics flood his thinking and he comes to see 'the decay of civilization as a result of a growing impotence in the traditional modern worldview of ethical world – and life – affirmation', and it became clear to him as to 'so many other people' that he had 'clung to that world-view from inner necessity, without troubling at all about how far it could be proved by thought'. Schweitzer goes on energetically to depict a worldview 'as an illusion within us which never ceases to stir our hearts yet never really gets dominion over us', but he does want that which 'offers itself to us as something desired from the depth of thought', that then can 'become spiritually our own' ([1931] 1933:182–83). Elsewhere he describes how, 'For months on end I lived in a continual state of mental excitement .... I was wandering in a thicket in which no path was to be found ... I was leaning with all my might against an iron door that would not yield', and he found no help in philosophy. He was 'exhausted and disheartened' not least because 'philosophy could be said never to have concerned itself with the problem of the connexion between civilization and world-view'. This was, he said, 'unexplored land' ([1931] 1933:184:85).

In Wilson's terms, here was a person in serious need of 'reassurance', and this is precisely where the gripping autobiographical narrative becomes inseparable from the mental-emotional and intrinsically mystical insight that came to him. He was in Africa, on a small steamer going upstream to visit a sick friend, sharing food with others because he had none himself, and covering many sheets of paper trying to work out his problems. These remained nothing more than disconnected sentences until, as he described it,

Late on the third day, at the very moment when, at sunset, we were making our way through a herd of hippopotamuses, there flashed through my mind, unforeseen and unsought, the phrase, 'Reverence for Life'. The iron door had yielded: the path in the thicket had become visible. Now I had found my way to the idea that in which world – and life – affirmation and ethics are contained side by side! Now I knew that the world-view of ethical world and life-affirmation with its ideals of civilization, is founded in thought.

Schweitzer is grasped by the notion that a person's ethical life is dependent upon life at large becoming 'sacred', whether 'of plants and animals' or other people, and coming when a person becomes devoted 'to all life that is in need of help' ([1931] 1933:188). This example of Schweitzer reveals strong theological and ethical tensions surrounding the meaning of existence in the life of one individual, but which emerged with the possibility of a worldview for many others. While it emerged before the later twentieth century's concern with environmentalism, it still carries powerful resonance within and outside traditional religious communities. It shows how an intuitive emotional capacity for merging personal life with a religious tradition can exert creative ideas, in his case with Christian doctrines of Christ and wider views of human engagement with the natural world.

Conclusion

From some basic approaches to a theoretical understanding of intuitive meaning-making and their potential application to religious, political, and natural contexts, this chapter has briefly indicated the significance of mystical elements in human life. Within a world of potential dangers and active perils, it has shown something of the resource that periods of conflict may prompt as people seek for reassurance.

12 Ideological worldview

Introduction

Acknowledging the worldviews already studied, the many more that could be embraced, and the limited extent of this book, this chapter brings together a selected number of further worldviews that do not depend upon supernatural or religious reference points but are frequently typified as secular. Sketched rather than analysed in detail, these depict distinctive individuals and ideologies whose rational bases involve their own emotional tone, organisational ethos, and aesthetic sense. These may be expressed in terms of beauty, love, ethical concern for others and for the earth itself, as well as an appreciation of the idea of truth and the lives given to its pursuit. These attributes need emphasis because religious traditions have often appropriated, patronised, and grounded them in personalised ideas of supernatural sources, most especially of God. This is a theoretically important point because many people find it easier to think of beauty, truth, or 'meaning' itself, as having some final source in 'someone' not totally unlike themselves, rather than having no personal anchorage. Something similar also often applies to grief and misfortune. If God, spirits, or the ancestors are in some way 'like' us, despite many statements also made about how different they are from us, many feel themselves safer amidst the many difficulties and occasional 'senseless' things that happen in life, than if no such lifeline exists. To reiterate this key point, the universe is an easier environment if it is believed to have been created by a rational and concerned deity or cosmic process possessing reasons, purposes, and goals explaining life's great complexity.

Secularities

However, once it is accepted that there is no divine source of things the human drive for meaning can pursue many other routes to understanding.

DOI: 10.4324/9781003242437-15

Some draw on studies of cosmology using mathematics, physics, and astronomy to discuss ideas of the origin of things. Others prefer philosophical, political, and economic theories to frame societies as intelligible contexts for life. Yet others find literature, poetry, art, music, and history to be aesthetic sources for a sense of life's depth.

Amidst these endeavours, cognitive science and evolutionary anthropology stand high in describing and offering interpretations for the widespread human preference for seeing agency in the world around us. Some find niche activities that create pockets of meaning for individuals, families, or small groups whether through gardens, pets, intimate relationships, or leisure events, as the final Ludic Worldviews chapter indicates. Whichever is the case, worldviews not only demand opportunity and resources but also need to match degrees of satisfaction demanded by people seeking some mastery of meaning.

Enchantment

Meaning-making is allied with the human property for curiosity set in contexts of unexplored physical and intellectual territories. Fostered by a particular attitude towards the unknown, curiosity entails a 'logic of enchantment' that excites and provokes 'new understandings of our world', even though it may 'diminish with familiarity' unless somehow replenished (Schneider, 1993:3). Doubtless such enchantment may be as much part of scientific discovery, including the discovery of very surprising behaviour of animals and plants cited in previous chapters. Certainly, re-stimulation of wonder underlies much religious worship, as does aesthetic pleasure in music or computer gaming. It may be that the current stimulus of environmental dangers is already driving science and engineering in their capacity to trigger curiosity and something analogous to 'enchantment', and that is important for mobilising many millions in support of eco-environmental shifts.

One key theoretical consideration of enchantment and its opposite – disenchantment – concerns Max Weber, already considered for his work on prophets and charisma that involve enchantments of their own. For Weber provided significant analysis of the shift from religiously enchanted western worldviews to the disenchanted domains of the Industrial Revolution from the later eighteenth into the early twentieth centuries. Many speak of these changes in population shifts and religious participation through theories of secularisation, but Weber speaks of it more as disenchantment. Key factors involved people moving from rural agricultural labour to dense urban dwellings with factory and mining work falling increasingly under the rational control of bureaucratic management and engineering precision.

While agricultural work and large-scale fishing were more subject to 'nature', weather, storm, seasons, flood, draught, and God, the industrial workplace was quite different. Weber's interest in the interplay between ideas and behaviour provided a way of discussing distinctive lifestyles and their framing worldviews, as when he aligned certain Protestant doctrinal beliefs with careful economic 'capitalist' lifestyle, giving rise to his idea of the Protestant Ethic as mentioned in chapter ten ([1904–5] 1976). Though lying beyond this book's scope, Weber's method could be analysed for today in terms of an ecological attitude partnering a low-carbon lifestyle of diet and travel within an environmental worldview.

Communism

Ideas of secularisation and disenchantment are probably best known within the ideological movement of Communism, certainly in terms of transforming major political–religious states. They underpinned the Russian Revolution (1917) leading to the era of the USSR, as also today's People's Republic of China, and that of Cuba. Karl Marx (1818–1883) and his theory of dialectical materialism, developed in different ways by other thinkers, reckoned that there were principles or laws of social development rooted in ideas of social class, revolution, and power exerted over workers by capitalist leaders. The goal of society was to remove these inequalities and redress the alienation of the worker from what was produced. Given Communism's Marxist and Leninist origins in the nineteenth century and its social conquest of Russia, it was immediately confronted by long-established forms of Christianity, and what began as a form of social–political protest inevitably involved the confrontation of ideology and theology.

As part of its transformation of a world framed by Orthodox Christianity, soviet leaders developed extensive forms of ritual-symbolism that sought to replace the full panoply of Orthodox Liturgy. Even the calendar by which time was measured was changed so as to dislocate major Orthodox religious festivals from the ordinary working of society (Binns, 1979, 1980, Lane, 1981). New ceremonies were devised for becoming members of the working class as well as for such ordinary events as first day at school. Such shifts clearly indicate the nature of worldviews as shared outlooks on life associated with celebration and the changing generations within families. One aspect of ideological worldviews lies in their politics-driven activity in regimenting their own population and also displaying military power in large-scale popular events. Submission of large populations and expansion into conquered territory reveal the distinctive nature of a political–ideological worldview. Expansion provides its own legitimation of the validity of the ideology itself. In some ways, this also parallels the Colonialisation previously witnessed in European nation-states, and also in a sense by the USA. Following the break-up of the USSR between 1988 and 1991 and, notably with President Putin from 2012, there has been a resurgence of the Russian Orthodox Church alongside the political regime, indicating something of the potential for change in dominant worldviews.

Secularisation and responses

Another approach to secularisation depicts a movement of religion from the public domain to that of private life. Religion becomes personal, leaving the public domain as a secular but usually not a secularist context. This complex argument needs detailed contextual analysis for each country. Some argue that many parts of western and northern Europe reflect such a mixed situation, while parts of the world manifest strong religious developments. Many parts of South America, for example, witnessed remarkable growth in Pentecostal-Charismatic Christianity from the later twentieth century.

From the 1960s, theories of secularisation have almost pre-occupied sociologists of religion, some following a trajectory from Weber (Wilson, 1966, Martin, 1978), while others set a shorter trajectory, as with Brown's notable work on the UK, pinpointing the mid-1960s as the critical starting point, not least because of the changing role of women in society and their decrease in religious participation (2001). Most of these sociological accounts make use of church attendance and membership figures as well as social surveys on belief and practice.

Some theologians also found secularisation of great interest, especially in the 1960s, partly prompted by sociological studies but especially by explicitly theological debates over the nature of faith, beliefs, and God. The American theologian Harvey Cox's *Secular City* (1966) saw the seeds of secularisation lying in the Jewish-Christian tradition itself. Following Weber's broad notion of disenchantment, Cox argued more specifically that the Genesis creation narratives laid the basis for disenchanting 'nature', the Exodus accounts drove a 'desacralization' of politics, and the Sinai Covenant between God and Israel did the same for a 'deconsecration' of cultural values. His rationale for this was that once a monotheism replaces polytheisms or other schemes of belief, social organisation and cultural values, its single focus becomes a more obvious target for subsequent disbelief. His stress on city life was important for secularisation in that it brought both cultural and historical relativity into play, assuming that when people live alongside those with quite different worldviews, they more easily question their own. Today such convictions certainly need reconsideration following the rise of migration and identity affirmation by groups living in relatively segregated communities.

By the beginning of the twenty-first century, a cluster of thinkers from biologist Richard Dawkins (2006) to philosopher Richard Grey (2018) began to engage with explicitly atheist accounts of a secularist worldview. Dawkins drives his argument from an original biological standpoint and offers a kind of scientific worldview wishing to eliminate 'religious' agents and, as my own conversation with him concerning death showed, this included the disliked thought that God might somehow oversee people's lives. Grey's considerations are more specifically rooted in philosophical reasoning.

The Sunday Assembly

Others who own similar ideas take practical action as with the relatively small number of people who set up their own form of ritual-symbolism in the Sunday Assembly. Founded in 2013 with a base in London and extensions across the globe, this involves largely middle-class and well-educated people. Often with previous Christian adherence, they gather on Sundays to enjoy a sense of community, with talks, music, songs, and refreshments. For some, this replaces what they had come to miss in life having left their previous religious groups as shown in a sociological study by Josh Bullock (2017). Some two centuries before this, the French philosopher Auguste Comte (1798–1857), often regarded as the originator of modern sociology, and proponent of Positivist Philosophy, created his own 'Religion of Humanity' involving the equivalent of ritual services, hymns, saint-like figures, apostles, and centres across the world, including India, and in Brazil (founded May 1881) where its online presence tells 'how to become a Positivist Church of Brazil member' (Positivist, 2021).

Yet others, typical of today's early twenty-first-century secular trends are neither 'congregational' nor militant in their more secularist lifestyle preference. Often described as 'spiritual but not religious', these individuals have been provided with a whole literature on 'Spirituality without God' – the subtitle to Comte-Sponville's *Atheist Spirituality* ([2006] 2008). More generally, Will Storr's account of 'how the west became self-obsessed' depicts seven designations of type of self (Dying, Tribal, Perfectible, Bad, Good, Special, Digital), each of which could be developed into its own worldview but, in contemporary society, generates issues of identity rather than destiny (Storr, 2017).

Conspiracy theory

As with Bullock's doctoral research on the Sunday Assembly, other doctoral research shows how conspiracy theories might qualify as a potential candidate for worldview status. Toseland's fieldwork-based observations led him to move beyond the popular and largely pejorative view of conspiracy theorists as deluded and dangerous, to speak of individuals united in a distinctive pattern of 'truth-seeking'. Under the dominant notion that the world is controlled by hidden élites, they speak of a kind of conversion enabling them to see through public conventions and identify those groups, while they begin to move in circles of like-minded persons attuned to different conspiracies. Toseland's two-year UK fieldwork involved intense engagement with groups concerned with alternative views of health, terrorist attacks, flat-earth beliefs, and the role of law. One of his key concerns pinpointed 'the recurring affirmation of the sacred character of humankind' (2019: Abstract). Such perspectives help sustain a compelling worldview for particular individuals, especially when reinforced by contact with similar minded people, and set against the different mindset of the public at large. However, these very small-scale groups do not gain any significant degree of purchase on society at large. Toseland's research, conducted between 2014 and 2016, pre-dated the Covid-19 pandemic beginning around 2020, and which would have added significant conspiracy-like materials generated around anti-vaccination groups, showing the latent 'conspiracy' power of individuals given appropriate triggers to align with conspiracy theories.

Gender–Identity

Sex and gender provide another perspective on worldviews and have assumed considerable public significance in the twenty-first century with both favourable and some negative consequences in political–legal–religious domains (de Groot and Morgan, 2014). Transformations in how biological sex, determined for the great majority at birth, has been discussed alongside gender as a question of how a person self-identifies with their ascribed sex-status has assumed enormous importance in terms of identity and availability of sex-linked social contexts. Indeed this reflects some recent sociological interest in ideas of fluidity of identity at large (Bauman, 2000). This issue echoes this book's 'idea–destiny' formulation of chapter three which highlighted the significance of emotion in transforming 'ideas' into values, and values as identity-framing forces. Just how individuals negotiate their sense of self in terms of how others might wish to define them, and in relation to the conventions of society that most other people simply appropriate, is an enormously complex issue. The biological, imaginative, and self-aware capacities of a person bring their own emotional forces to the social ideas of boy–girl and woman–man binary classifications and influence people's values and identity preferences. The presence of the internet now allows access to a wide field of like-minded or like-sensed people, allowing groups to emerge from isolated individuals. The increasingly familiar acronym of L.G.B.T.Q.I.A.+ aligns lesbian, gay, bisexual, transgender, queer, intersex, and asexual identities, while also allowing (+) for further categories such as those questioning (Q) their position, or pansexual (Pan) and open to all other categories, as well as those who see themselves as an Ally of all such groups. This diversity of gender-identity is especially important for worldview studies because it highlights how dynamic networks host individuals for whom their sexual and gender identities are of enormous if not paramount importance. In modern societies, there are very many groups whose life-focus through sexuality and identity constitutes their prime worldview, and they may find social circles in which to realise this, even though their wider society and its more dominant worldview may differ quite considerably. This highlights the interplay of personal, group, and total-social perspectives that confront anyone engaged in worldview studies. For many societies and nation-states issues of traditional religion have tended to play an enormous part in confronting and contradicting these issues, on the basis that divine creations are well ordered, with the male–female binary divide part of that holy order. Only in the twenty-first century are some traditions engaging more openly with the issues involved, often under the influence of Human Rights legislation.

Human Rights

The major framework that includes issues of sexuality and gender, as well as social class, and access to life-fulfilling and not depleting contexts, is that of Human Rights, especially as framed by the Universal Declaration of Human Rights, an instrument of the 1948 United Nations General Assembly. This milestone document set out in its International Bill of Human Rights (Fact Sheet No.2. (Rev.1)):

> All human beings are born free and equal in dignity and rights.
> They are endowed with reason and conscience and should act towards one another in a spirit of brotherhood.

While these ideals comprise their own form of high-order worldview, taking ethical and philosophical–political positions on to a universal stage, the Declaration shows the significant complexity of the idea of worldview. For what nations may reckon they want to see and whether they implement it are two different things.

Indifference

This issue of implementation applies to any of the worldviews cited in this book, and relates to the topic of simple indifference (Davies, 2017:378–81). Most worldviews extend from high-order assertions of 'reality', perhaps, maintained by elites, through to ordinary people who may have some sense of them, and act upon that at certain times and places, while also having the capacity for indifference at other times. This is an issue besetting many forms of less than nuanced social survey work on religious beliefs and adherence, not least because of shifting adherence and levels of institutional commitment across a person's life-course. One interesting aspect of indifference and commitment arises in connection with people's basic self-interest, as in welfare and healthcare.

The Welfare State and UK National Health Service

It makes sense to align this brief section on welfare and health with Human Rights, indeed they belong together as far as people's ordinary perspectives are concerned, while always recognising the diversity evident in different countries. As far as the UK is concerned, The National Health Service (NHS) is part of the Welfare State, and has, from 1948 onwards, increasingly become its own kind of worldview central to political debate as to the life-experience of the public. In some respects, it functions as the driver of a British worldview, mobilising ideas of justice, fairness, and the value of 'life' itself (Davies, 2015:98–101). Increasing numbers of research projects, especially in developed societies, explore the ways 'religion and welfare systems provide competing "insurance policies", and indirectly trace competing dynamics between worldviews' (Granqvist, 2020:304–10).

Environmentalism

Although environmentalism has been specifically discussed in previous chapters, it is pinpointed here because its ideological, scientific, and ethical drivers now engage global concern. This is marked by the international assembly of many of the world's political leaders in November 2021 in Glasgow. While sharing much in a 'natural worldview', it is increasingly a political issue of high order while also attracting interest from religious leaders. This is another example of the complexity of 'worldview' ideas, and especially of how a worldview both demands and excites interest from all levels of a society as it makes practical demands on pragmatic ways of life including domestic heating and cooling, local and international travel, food supplies, and potential waves of migration.

Conclusion

These diverse groups not only indicate the significance of philosophical, ecological, and other drivers in generating and developing worldviews but also the complexity involved in thinking about worldviews, whether as high-, mid-, or low-range phenomena. These cases demonstrate the similarities and differences between the meaning-making pursued by secular and religious means, and also prepare the way for the final chapter's exploration of an even greater diversity of behaviours that can be summarised within a Ludic Worldview.

13 Ludic worldview

Introduction

When the Dutch historian Johan Huizinga (1872–1945) published *Homo Ludens* in the 1930s, he stimulated an ongoing interest in the playful properties of humans (Huizinga, [1930] 1950). Not much later, the child psychologist D. W. Winnicott (1896–1971) developed his theory of play as a universal feature of child development and of healthy adult life ([1971] 1991:51–85). More recently some scholars have also approached religion in terms of 'pleasure and fun' (Jespers et al. 2018).

These signposts to play are followed up here through cases that set 'play' or the ludic aspect of life (Latin *ludo* – 'I play') as a candidate for worldview status, or at least as a mid-range theory for other worldview activities such as comedy, sport, gambling, internet gaming, and Christmas. These specially selected phenomena embrace the game-like features of exploration, excitement, pleasure, and the rule-based and goal-seeking behaviours of shared endeavour. While each offers a partial perspective on life, taken together, they embrace a wide perspective on existence. Moreover, while the 'ludic' element provides an insight into and a means of research on religious and worldview studies, it also raises ethical aspects of fieldwork.

Droogers, van Harskamp: Worldview and Religious Studies

Developing Huizinga's work, André Droogers and Anton van Harskamp have edited a key text *Methods for the Study of Religious Change* (2014) that has much influenced this present study as evident in their crucial subtitle – *From Religious Studies to Worldview Studies*. Of special importance is their notion of 'methodological ludism' which proposes that 'the human gift for play' is something basic to the very process of scholarly analysis (2014:5, 62). At first this may sound odd since 'play' is often seen as

DOI: 10.4324/9781003242437-16

separate from 'serious' thinking. Their point, however, is that if play is 'the capacity to deal simultaneously and subjectively with two or more ways of classifying reality', then it resembles the process of a person studying social events and being part of ongoing events while 'yet standing apart' and studying it (2014:69–70). Fieldworkers pursuing participant-observation methods require time to develop the skills demanded by this. Indeed, Droogers and van Harskamp are alert to the difficulties some researchers encounter over their sense of identity (2014:77), an issue also taken up in this book's conclusion.

Playing with ideas

Very similar to Droogers and van Harskamp's use of ludic capacities to analyse actual participation in activities is the more abstract capacity to 'play' with ideas when approaching issues in a 'what if' kind of way. Much creative thinking in this open-ended fashion often generates new insights across many fields of study. Moreover, many see adult creativity as a retention of the childhood capacity for play as, for example, with Raymond Moody who developed the study of Near Death Experiences (NDE) that became widely popular through accounts of those who had been revived after having been 'clinically' dead. These reported largely positive and joyous experiences of being 'out of the body', travelling through tunnels of light, encountering loving afterlife figures who tell them to go back to their earth-life. On recovering, they frequently spoke of having lost any fear of dying.

Such events obviously raise the question of what such NDE means and in *The Last Laugh* (1999), Moody not only acknowledges the difficulties involved in that assessment but also criticises three groups for their overly simplistic interpretations. Parapsychologists used NDE too easily to prove an afterlife or soul; sceptical scientists with reductionist explanations of chemical shifts in the brain; and Fundamentalist Christians who use biblical texts to attack the very idea of NDE. Moody preferred a more open appreciation of NDE that echoed a creative playing with these very unusual life experiences. Though his own research methods have received much criticism, he retains and advocates the curiosity of play.

Sport

A more immediately obvious and direct application of play lies in the field of sport. Some see sport as a cultural side-line and leisure aspect of life entertained within other worldviews, and it can certainly be argued that sports are but one commerce-driven aspect of consumerism within societies that are, in themselves, ideologically driven. Certainly, Russia, China, the USA, India, Pakistan, and many other countries use 'sport' not only as part of their internal leisure, but also as external means of state-assertion. Scholars have, for example, analysed the importance of football in developing a national focus in Germany following its defeat in the Second World War (Krauss, 2003), as well as showing how sports, including dance, express national and gender identities (Dyck and Archetti, 2003).

Just who wins the Olympic Games, international football matches, or other athletic ventures is something of real concern for some countries, as is their musical performance on the international stage. Deep commitments are attached to teams and players, and to the ritual and art-forms of play. The Olympic Games movement offers its own rationale for international relationships embracing the excellence of human bodies subjected to competition according to set rules. Cheating, especially doping, is formally acknowledged as reprehensible and being a 'good sport' is praised. In some ways, this competitive world reveals an intensification of ordinary rule-based living. Indeed, it is easy to describe some fans as dedicated, echoing religious language of devotion, and accounting for the importance of sport and shared fandom in a person's life and as part of a worldview of its own.

Comedy

One feature of twenty-first-century life, at least in the UK, concerns comedy, especially stand-up comedians performing on television, social media, and to immense public arenas across the country and beyond. Although their 'take' on public life maps a diversity of cynical, ironic, sexual, political, or simply funny comments on ordinary life situations, they differ markedly from the political satire of the 1960s in the much watched television programme 'That Was the Week That Was'. By the 2020s, comedy is more mainstream and runs across many genres, some comedians even couple with scientists in hybrid ventures, while others are panellists jesting with quiz-like questions. If there is some kind of worldview projected in these, it seems to favour a lightness of life amongst celebrities open to playfully talking about themselves, albeit in a culture where some individuals very easily self-identify as victims or take offence at how they are treated by others.

Gambling, internet gaming, and play

Another aspect of the playful-ludic outlook lies in gambling, from betting-shops and online casino gambling through to national and international lotteries. Inviting emotions of excitement and anticipating good fortune amidst a more boring lifestyle such gambling almost resembles the ethos of the stand-up comedian; the fun depicting ordinariness parallels the hope to break-free from the mundane. The making of a millionaire by sheer chance offers an interesting insight into some people's longings, aspirations, and the worldview within which this occurs. When Falk and Mäenpiää ([1997] 1999) studied 'lottery millionaires', they revealed the troubles as well as pleasures involved in winning, notably when the winner's response some-times prompts the thought that random misfortune might befall them just as easily as good luck. Still, what emerges in their research is the place of hope in people's lives, and this perhaps is its own hallmark of a ludic worldview that may not be too far removed from the desire for changed circumstances found in Internet activities that create imaginative worlds in which individuals generate avatars of themselves to engage in rule-controlled play amidst self-architected environments. Film and narrative of many kinds are playful forms of making sense of the world.

Christmas

Christmas can be taken as a final example of a ludic perspective within cultures of Christian heritage. Theoretical analyses of Christmas integrate society-wide celebration, active participation of families, the 'performance' of parenting, much expression of reciprocity through gifts, emphasis on children within extended family life, and some sense of a transcendent 'spirit of Christmas'. Two of the 'plays' within the Season's festivities speak to all of these features, that of the Christian Nativity Scene telling the birth of Jesus as a divine and saving gift to humanity – played out through schools, civic and commercial contexts, as well as churches, and that of Father Christmas, the gift-bringer and imaginative focus of childhood wonder. The way parents and teenage siblings foster 'belief' in Father Christmas is itself a remarkable example of ludism as imaginative pretence aimed at fostering joy.

Conclusion

These cases illustrate how some human emotions are intensified in specific contexts and forms. Relatively untrammelled from the mundane organisation of dutiful life, they point to the role of hope associated with worship, festivals, pilgrimages, and the cultural creativity of worldviews at large. However, for the researcher, as this chapter's Introduction mentioned, field-work inevitably involves ethical and identity-survival features. Just how 'ludic' can research be? Can a person 'play the cultural game' while also analysing it, and remaining true to their own identity? What reservations or sacrifices might a researcher need to make when participating in and coming to 'understand' what is going on? Perhaps personal change is integral to this form of academic study. Here key ethical issues on authenticity and personal life-commitments need deep consideration lying beyond the scope of this book.

14 Seeing and seeing-through worldviews

Introduction

So it is that with many issues remaining untouched in this very provisional attempt at Worldview Religious Studies this final chapter offers no immediate 'conclusion'. Instead, it pursues two topics that stand as signposts to the future: one highlights the potential tonalities of worldviews, and the other, the rather enigmatic topic of seeing and seeing-through worldviews.

Worldviews, ethos, and tone

The first simply records this book's pursuit of the familiar theme of meaning-making with its stress on the alignment of emotional and cognitive processes in identity-formation and in terms of the notion of destiny, all directed towards an exploratory typology of worldviews (Davies, 1984, Tomlinson and Engelke, 2006). This has emphasised selected social-scientific topics without ignoring aspects of the arts, humanities, and theological studies. Some quite unfamiliar topics have been added to very familiar themes of Religious Studies with the intention of stimulating discussion and signposting directions of further creative thought. One of the more significant of these concerns the emotional tones of different groups related to Weber, Bateson, and Geertz on mood and ethos. Geertz is especially important for this book because his understanding of emotional tone sustains what is, effectively, a working definition of worldview, one that embraces many key themes of this book.

> A people's ethos is the tone, character, and quality of their life, its moral and aesthetic style and mood: it is the underlying attitude towards themselves and their world that life reflects. Their world-view is the picture of the way things, in sheer actuality are, their concept of nature, of self, of society.
>
> (1957:421)

DOI: 10.4324/9781003242437-17

This requires a slight rearrangement of elements to depict a general model identifying a worldview as a picture of the way things are for a group, including their concept of nature, self, and society; their style, mood, and preferred ethos embracing a tone, character, and quality of life. While this book may have achieved something in its proposed typology of worldviews and variety of theories and conceptual tools that help analyse the dynamic processes of 'the way things are' in life, it has also expressed the specific need for more work on the emotional tonality of worldviews, something that will demand the interplay of the psychology and sociology of emotions, musical and performance theory, as well as aesthetics. Although only the smallest of steps have been taken in that direction, just how tonal scales might embrace high, mid, and low ranges of different worldviews awaits future analysis.

Seeing, seeing-through, and 'seeing-through'

The second, and concluding, topic of this study concerns what can be summarised in the multi-vocal phrase 'seeing and seeing through'. From childhood, it is natural to 'see' things through our culture's classification of reality that provides our passage into adult identity in a shared worldview. But then, for a small minority, the formal comparative study of religions or worldviews offers new ways of 'seeing' things, one that offers a distinctively distanced perspective. Here, the idioms of 'seeing', 'insight', and the more culturally nuanced notion of the 'gaze', are highly relevant, and even have their own academic niche (Sauer, 2014). One consequence of such an entry into 'other' worldviews is that it may trigger a reflexive response, whether of excitement or even of defence. Previously taken for granted values, beliefs, identities, and even destiny, may be questioned, especially if our ordinary worldview claims religious uniqueness and truthfulness.

This is where someone may get a sense of 'seeing-through' what had once appeared so solid. Many kinds of study that prompt us to be human-curious often make us self-aware in such new ways. And while this can be a largely positive and highly adaptive experience, it can also be profoundly problematic if it brings a person to question their own outlook on life in a way that is sensed as seriously undermining their previously firm identity. There is no easy resolution to this dynamic process of initial seeing our world in one way, then perhaps seeing-through its claim to exclusivity when set alongside other 'unique' perspectives. For some, this can prompt a loss of confidence in the worldview of their home community, and encourage an overwhelming sense of the relativity or even loss of ideas of 'truth'. Some others, by contrast, certainly understand this relativity of worldviews but come to accept the wisdom of explicitly committing themselves to what they had once taken for granted albeit in a modified fashion. While this may afford a higher-order sense of 'meaning' in the world while prompting a voluntary, insightful, commitment to the way things are, it can also prompt a desire to abandon that worldview or even foster the creation of a new worldview.

Bibliography

Aberbach, D. (1996) *Charisma in Politics, Religion and the Media*. London: McMillan.
Alter, R. (1981) *The Art of Biblical Narrative*. New York: Basic Books, HarperCollins.
Asma, S. T. (2018) *Why We Need Religion*. Oxford: Oxford University Press.
Atran, S. (2002) *In Gods We Trust: The Evolutionary Landscape of Religion*. Oxford: Oxford University Press.
Attenborough, D. (2021) *The Living Planet*. London: HarperCollins.
Augustine (1945) *The City of God*. Introduction by Sir Ernest Barker. London: Dent and Sons.
Balcombe, J. (2016) *What a Fish Knows: The Inner Lives of Our Underwater Cousins*. One World Books.
Barker, E. (1945) 'Introduction'. *The City of God, St Augustine*. London: Dent. pp. vii–xxxviii.
Bateson, G. ([1936] 1958) *Naven*. Stanford, CA: Stanford University Press.
Bauman, Z. (1992) *Mortality, Immortality*. London: Polity Press.
Bauman, Z. (2000) *Liquid Modernity*. Cambridge: Polity.
Beiler, K. J., Durall, D. M., Simard, S. W., Maxwell, S. A., and A. M. Kretzer (2010) 'Mapping the wood-wide web: Mycorrhizal networks link multiple Douglas-fir cohorts'. *New Phytologist*, 192(3): 689–698.
Benson H. and M. Z. Klipper (1975) *The Relaxation Response*. New York: William Morrow.
Berger, P. (1969) *The Social Reality of Religion*. London: Penguin Books.
Binns, C. (1979) 'The changing face of power: Revolution and accommodation in the development of the Soviet ceremonial system 1'. *Journal of the Royal Anthropological Institute*, 14(4): 585–606.
Binns, C. (1980) 'The changing face of power: Revolution and accommodation in the development of the Soviet ceremonial system 2'. *Journal of the Royal Anthropological Institute*, 15(1): 170–87.
Bostridge. I. (2015) *Schubert's Winter Journey, Anatomy of an Obsession*. London: Faber and Faber.
Boyer, P. (ed.) (1993) *Cognitive Aspects of Ritual Symbols*. Cambridge: Cambridge University Press.
Boyer, P. (2001) *Religion Explained: The Evolutionary Origins of Religious Thought*. New York: Basic Books.

Brown, C. (2001) *The Death of Christian Britain: Understanding Secularisation 1800–2000*. London: Routledge.

Bullock, J. (2017) *The Sociology of the Sunday Assembly: 'Belonging Without Believing' in a PostChristian Context*. Doctoral dissertation, Kingston University, London.

Chater, M. and L. Donnellan (2020) 'What do we mean by worldviews?'. *Reforming RE. Power and Knowledge in a Worldviews Curriculum*. (ed.) M. Chater. Woodbridge: John Catt Educational. pp. 115–147.

Childs, D. (2008) *Growing Remembrance: The Story of The National Memorial Arboretum*. Lichfield: National Memorial Arboretum.

Christopher, K. (2020) 'Towards a Worldviews curriculum: Managing content, ensuring progression'. *Reforming RE. Power and Knowledge in a Worldviews Curriculum*. (ed.) M. Chater. Woodbridge: John Catt Educational. pp.197–206.

Comte-Sponville, A. ([2006] 2008) *The Book of Atheist Spirituality*. Translated by N. Huston. London: Bantam Books.

Cosgrove, D. and S. Daniels (1988) *The Iconography of Landscape*. Cambridge: Cambridge University Press.

Cox, H. (1966) *The Secular City*. New York: Macmillan.

Csikszentmihalyi, M. ([1974] 1991) *Flow, The Psychology of Optimal Experience*. New York: Harper Perennial.

Dallos, R. (2004) 'Attachment narrative therapy: Integrating ideas from narrative and attachment theory in systematic family therapy and eating disorders'. *Journal of Family Therapy*, 26(1): 40–65.

Davies, D. J. (1984) *Meaning and Salvation in Religious Studies*. Leiden: Brill.

Davies, D. J. (1994) 'Introduction: Raising the issues'. *Human Nature and Destiny*. (eds.) J. Holm and J. Bowker. London, New York: Pinter Publisher. pp. 1–8.

Davies, D. J. (1997) 'Human nature and destiny'. *Themes and Issues in Christianity*. (eds.) D. J. Davies with C. Drury. London. Cassell. pp. 63–93.

Davies, D. J. (2000) *The Mormon Culture of Salvation*. Aldershot: Ashgate.

Davies, D. J. (2002) *Anthropology and Theology*. Oxford: Berg.

Davies, D. J. (2004) 'Purity, spirit and reciprocity in the acts of the apostles'. *Anthropology and Biblical Studies*. (eds.) L. J. Lawrence and M. Aguilar. pp. 259–280.

Davies, D. J. (2008) 'Cultural intensification: A theory for religion'. *Religion and the Individual*. (ed.) A. Day. Aldershot: Ashgate. pp. 7–18.

Davies, D. J. (2011) *Emotion, Identity, and Religion: Hope, Reciprocity and Otherness*. Oxford: Oxford University Press.

Davies, D. J. (2015) *Mors Britannica: Lifestyle and Death-Style in Britain Today*. Oxford: Oxford University Press.

Davies, D. J. (2017) *Death, Ritual and Belief: The Rhetoric of Funerary Rites*. London: Bloomsbury.

Davies, D. J. and M. Guest (2007) *Bishops, Wives and Children, Spiritual Capital Across the Generations*. Aldershot: Ashgate.

Davies, D. J. and D. Northam-Jones (2012) 'The sea of faith: Exemplifying transformed retention'. *Religion and Knowledge, Sociological Perspectives*. (eds.) M. Guest and E. Arweck. London, Farnham: Ashgate. pp. 227–246.

Davies, D. J. and H. Rumble (2012) *Natural Burial: Traditional-Secular Spiritualities and Funeral Innovation*. London: Continuum.

Dawkins, R. (2006) *The God Delusion*. Boston, NY: Houghton Mifflin Co.

Dawson, L. L. (ed.) (1998) *Cults in Context, Readings in the Study of New Religious Movements*. London: Transaction Publishers.

Descola, P. ([2005] 2013) *Beyond Nature and Culture*. Translated by J. Lloyd. London: University of Chicago Press.

Dilthey, W. (1911) *Die Typen der Welstanschauung und inhre Ausbildung in den Metaphysischen Systemen*. Berlin: Reichl.

Douglas, M. (1966) *Purity and Danger*. London: Routledge and Kegan Paul.

Douglas, M. (1970) *Natural Symbols*. London: Pelican Books.

Droogers, A. and A. van Harskamp. (2014) *Methods for the Study of Religious Change: From Religious Studies to Worldview Studies*. Sheffield: Equinox.

Durkheim, E. (1915) *The Elementary Forms of the Religious Life*. Translated by J. W. Swain. London: Allen & Unwin.

Duschinsky, R. Shnall, S. and D. H. Weiss (2016) *Purity and Danger: New Perspectives*. London: Routledge.

Eliade, M. (1964) *Shamanism: Archaic Techniques of Ecstasy*. London: Penguin Books.

Enstedt, D., Larsson, G., and T. T. Mantsinen (eds.) (2020) *Handbook on Leaving Religion*. Leiden: Brill.

Evans, J. (2014) *God's Trees, Trees, forests and wood in the Bible*. Leominster: Day.

Evans-Pritchard, E. E. (1965) *Theories of Primitive Religion*. Oxford: Clarendon Press.

Falk, P. and P. Mäenpiää (1999) *Hitting the Jackpot, Lives of Lottery Millionaires*. Oxford: Berg.

Fitzgerald, T. (2000) *The Ideology of Religious Studies*. Oxford: Oxford University Press.

Freud, S. (1960) *Totem and Taboo*. London: Routledge and Kegan Paul.

Freud, S. (1973) *New Introductory Lectures on Psychoanalysis. The Pelican Freud Library*, Volume 2. Translated by J. Strachey, edited by J. Strachey, assisted by A. Richards. Harmondsworth, UK: Penguin Books.

Geertz, C. (1957, Winter) 'Ethos, world-view and the analysis of sacred symbols'. *The Antioch Review*, 17(4): 421–437. https://doi.org/10.2307/4609997.

Geertz, C. (1993) *The Interpretation of Cultures: Selected Essays*. London: Fontana.

Gillis, K. and B. Gatersleben (2015) 'A review of psychological literature on the health and wellbeing benefits of biophilic design'. *Buildings*, 5(3): 948–963.

Godelier, M. (1999) *The Enigma of the Gift*. Oxford: Blackwell.

Godfrey-Smith, P. (2016) *Other Minds: The Octopus and the Evolution of Intelligent Life*. London: HarperCollins.

Goodhart, D. (2017) *The Road to Somewhere: The Populist Revolt and the Future of Politics*. London: Hurst and Company.

Gore, A. (2006) *An Inconvenient Truth. The Planetary Emergency of Global Warming and What We Can Do About It*. New York: Rodale.

Granqvist, P. (2020) *Attachment in Religion and Spirituality*. New York: Guilford Press.

Greet, J. de and S. Morgan (2014) *Sex, Gender and the Sacred, Reconfiguring Religion in Gender History.* Oxford: WILEY Blackwell.

Grey, R. (2018) *Seven Types of Atheism.* London: Allen Lane.

Grimes, R. L (1990) *Ritual Criticism: Case Studies in its Practice, Essays on its Theory.* Columbia, SC: University of South Carolina Press.

Guidebook, Explore, Discover, Remember. (2017) Alrewas, Staffordshire: National Memorial Arboretum.

Haddon, A. C. (1910) *History of Anthropology.* London: Watts and Co.

Harvey, P. (2002) *Introduction to Buddhist Ethics: Foundations, Values, and Issues.* Oxford: Oxford University Press.

Hoggart, R. (1995) *The Way We Live Now.* London: Pimlico.

Holm, J. with J. Bowker (eds.) (1994) *Human Nature and Destiny.* London, New York: Pinter Publisher.

Hubert, H. and M. Mauss ([1899] 1964) *Sacrifice its Nature and Function.* Translated by W. D. Halls. London: Cohen and West.

Huizinga, J. (1950) *Homo Ludens, A Study of the Play-element in Culture.* New York: Roy Publishers.

Jackson, S. T. and L. D. Walls (2014) *Views of Nature: Alexander von Humbolt.* Chicago, IL: University of Chicago Press.

Jakobsen, M. D. (1999) *Shamanism.* Oxford: Berghahn.

Jespers, F., van Nieuwkerk, and P. van der Velde. (2018) *Enjoying Religion. Pleasure and Fun in Established and New Religious Movements.* London: Lexington Books.

Kasler, D. (1988) *Max Weber: An Introduction to his Life and Work.* Cambridge: Polity Press.

Kay, J. and M. King (2020) *Radical Uncertainty, Decision-making for an Unknowable Future.* London: Bridge Street Press.

Keane, A. H. (1908) *The World's Peoples.* London: Hutchinson and Co.

Keller, B. and H. Streib (2013) 'Faith development, religious styles and biographical narratives: Methodological perspectives'. *Journal of Empirical Theology,* 26(2013): 1–21.

Knabb, J. J. and M. Y. Emerson. (2013) '"I will be your God and you will be my People": Attachment theory and the grand narrative of scripture'. *Pastoral Psychology,* 62(6): 827–841.

Kotoh, T. (1992) 'Language and silence: Self-inquiry in Heidegger and Zen'. *Martin Heidegger, Critical Assessments.* (ed.) C. Macann. London: Routledge.

Krauss, W. (2003) 'Football, nation and identity: German miracles in the postwar era'. *Sport, Dance and Embodied Identities'.* (eds.) N. Dyck and E. P. Archetti. Oxford: Berg. pp. 197–215.

Lane, C. (1981) *The Rites of Rulers: Ritual in Industrial Society.* Cambridge: Cambridge University Press.

Lee, L. (2014) 'Secular or nonreligious? Investigating and interpreting generic 'not religious' categories and populations'. *Religion,* 44(3): 466–482.

Lévi-Strauss, C. (1962) *Totemism.* London: Merlin Press.

Levi-Strauss, C. ([1958] 1963) *Structural Anthropology.* London: Allen Lane.

Lienhardt, G. (1961) *Divinity and Experience: The Religion of the Dinka.* Oxford: Clarendon Press.

Loetz, C. Muller, J. Frick, E., and Y. Peterson (2013) 'Attachment theory and spirituality. Two threads converging in palliative care'. *Evidence-Based Complementary and Alternative Medicine*, 2013: 740291. doi: 10.1155/2013/740291

Lovelock, J. (1979) *Gaia: A new look at life on Earth*. Oxford: Oxford University Press.

Lovelock, J. (2019) *Novacene: The Coming of Age of Hyper Intelligence*. London: Allen Land, Penguin Books.

Malinowski, B. ([1948] 1974) *Magic, Science, and Religion*. London: Souvenir Press.

Martin, D. (1978) *A General Theory of Secularization*. Oxford: Blackwells.

McCauley, R. N. and E. T. Lawson (2002) *Bringing Ritual to Mind. Psychological Foundations of Cultural Forms*. Cambridge: Cambridge University Press.

Miller, D. (2008) *The Comfort of Things*. Cambridge: Polity Press.

Miller, D. (2010) *Stuff*. Cambridge Polity Press.

Mol, H. (1976) *Identity and the Sacred: A sketch for a new social-scientific theory of religion*. Oxford: Basil Blackwell.

Moody, R. (1999) *The Last Laugh: A new philosophy of near-death experiences, apparitions and the para-normal*. Charlottesville, VA: Hampton Roads Pub.

Obeyesekere, G. (1968) 'Theodicy, Sin and Salvation in a Sociology of Buddhism'. *Dialectic in Practical Religion*. (ed.) E. R. Leach. Cambridge: Cambridge University Press.

Otto, R. (1924) *The Idea of the Holy*. Translated by J. H. Harvey. Oxford: Oxford University Press.

Park, C. W. (2010) *Cultural Blending in Korean Death Rites*. London: Continuum.

Parsons, T. 'Introduction'. *The Sociology of Religion*. Translated by Ephraim Fischoff, with Introduction by Talcott Parsons. London: Methuen and Co.

Partridge, C. (2015) *Mortality and Music, Popular Music and the Awareness of Death*. London: Bloomsbury.

Positivist (2021) See www.igrejapositivistabrasil.org.br/english/ accessed 06/10/2021.

Rappaport, R. A. (1999) *Ritual and Religion in the Making of Humanity*. Cambridge: Cambridge University Press.

Raud, R. (2021) *Asian Worldviews: Religions, Philosophies and Political Theories*. Hoboken, NJ: Wiley-Blackwell.

Said, E. W. ([1978] 2003) *Orientalism*. London: Penguin Books.

Sauer, M. M. (2014) 'Architecture of desire: Mediating the female gaze in the medieval English anchorhold'. *Sex, Gender and the Sacred, Reconfiguring Religion in Gender History*. (eds.) Joanna de Groot and Sue Morgan. Oxford: Wiley Blackwell. pp. 150–169.

Scheider, M. A. (1993) *Culture and Enchantment*. Chicago, IL: University of Chicago Press.

Schleiermacher, F. ([1806] 1958) *On Religion, Speeches to Its Cultured Despisers*. New York: Harper and Row.

Schweitzer, A. ([1901] 1914) *The Mystery of the Kingdom of God*. London: Adam and Charles Black.

Schweitzer, A. ([1906] 2005) *The Quest for the Historical Jesus*. London: Dover.

Schweitzer, A. ([1931] 1933) *Albert Schweitzer My Life and Thought, An Autobiography*. London: Allen and Unwin Ltd.

Schweitzer, A. ([1931] 1953) *The Mysticism of Paul the Apostle*. London: Adam and Charles Black.

Schweitzer, A. ([1966] 1974) *Reverence for Life*. London: SPCK.

Seybold, K. S. (2007) *Neuroscience, Psychology and Religion*. Aldershot: Ashgate.

Simard, S. W., Perry, D. A., Jones, M. D., Myrold, D. M., Durall, D. M., and Molina, R. (1997) 'Net transfer of carbon between ectomycorrhizal tree species in the field'. *Nature*, 388: 579–582.

Smart, N. (1996) *Dimensions of the Sacred: An Anatomy of the World's Beliefs*. London: HarperCollins.

Smith, W. R. (1994) *The Religion of the Semites*. Edinburgh: A & C Black.

Sperber, D. (1975) *Rethinking Symbolism*. Cambridge: Cambridge University Press.

Spitzer, M. (2021) *The Musical Human, A History of Life on Earth*. London: Bloomsbury.

Storr, A. (1997) *Feet of Clay: A Study of Gurus*. London: HarperCollins.

Storr, W. (2017) *Selfie, How the West Became Self-obsessed*. London: Picador.

Suriano, M. (2018) *A History of Death in the Hebrew Bible*. Oxford: Oxford University Press.

Tambiah, S. J. (1968) 'The Ideology of Merit and the Social Correlates of Buddhism in a Thai Village'. *Dialectic in Practical Religion*. (ed.) E. Leach. Cambridge: Cambridge University Press.

Taves, A. (1999) *Fits, Trances and Visions: Experiencing Religion and Exploring Experience from Wesley to James*. Princeton, NJ: Princeton University Press.

Tomlinson, M. and M. Engelke. (2006) 'Meaning, Anthropology, Christianity'. *The Limits of Meaning, Case Studies in the Anthropology of Christianity*. (eds.) M. Engelke and M. Tomlinson. Oxford: Berghahn Books. pp. 1–37.

Toseland, N. R. E. (2019) *Truth, "Conspiracy Theorists" and Theories: An Ethnographic Study of "Truth-Seeking" in Contemporary Britain'*. Doctoral Dissertation, University of Durham.

Tremlin, T. (2006) *Minds and Gods: The Cognitive Foundations of Religion*. Oxford: Oxford University Press.

Universal Declaration of Human Rights (art. 1), adopted by General Assembly resolution 217 A (III) of 10 December 1948. United Nations.

Urubshurow, V. K. (2008) *Introducing World Religions*. London: Routledge.

Weber, M. ([1922] 1966) *The Sociology of Religion*. Translated by Ephraim Fischoff, with Introduction by Talcott Parsons. London: Methuen and Co.

Weber, M. (1976) *The Protestant Ethic and the Spirit of Capitalism*. Translated by Talcott Parsons. London: Allen and Unwin.

Williams, J. M. G. (2011) *Mindfulness*. London: Piatkus.

Williams, P. and A. W. A. Tribe (2000) *Buddhist Thought*. London: Routledge.

Williams, R. (1981) *Culture*. Glasgow: William Collins.

Wilson, B. R. (1970) *Religious Sects*. World University Library.

Wilson, B. R. (1966) *Religion in Secular Society*. London: Pelican.

Wilson, B. R. (1973) *Magic and the Millennium*. London: Heinemann.

Winnicott, D. W. ([1971] 1991) *Playing and Reality*. London: Routledge.

Wohlleben, P. (2017) *The Hidden Life of Trees: What they Feel and How they Communicate*. London: William Collins.

Wulf, A. (2008) *The Brother Gardeners, Botany, Empire and the Birth of an Obsession*. London: Windmill Books.

Wyschogrod, E. (1998) 'Value'. In *Critical Terms for Religious Studies*. Edited by Mark C. Taylor. Chicago, IL: University of Chicago Press. pp. 365–382.

Yates, T. (2004) *The Expansion of Christianity*. Oxford: Lion Publishing.

Young, K. (2002) 'The Memory of the Flesh'. *Body and Society*, 8(3): 25–48.

Index

Printed in Great Britain
by Amazon